Capital Campaigns

Capital Campaigns

A Guide for Board Members and Others Who Aren't Professional Fundraisers but Who Will Be the Heroes Who Create a Better Community

How your hospital, civic organization, social or human service agency, museum, school, university, community college, theater, church, musical group, or just about any not-for-profit organization can raise $1 million to $100 million to build a new building, expand your current building, create an endowment, or otherwise move to the next level

Stuart R. Grover, Ph.D.

iUniverse, Inc.
New York Lincoln Shanghai

Capital Campaigns
A Guide for Board Members and Others Who Aren't Professional Fundraisers but Who Will Be the Heroes Who Create a Better Community

Copyright © 2006 by Stuart R. Grover

iUniverse books may be ordered through booksellers or by contacting:

iUniverse
2021 Pine Lake Road, Suite 100
Lincoln, NE 68512
www.iuniverse.com
1-800-Authors (1-800-288-4677)

ISBN-13: 978-0-595-41472-7 (pbk)
ISBN-13: 978-0-595-67912-6 (cloth)
ISBN-13: 978-0-595-85821-7 (ebk)
ISBN-10: 0-595-41472-9 (pbk)
ISBN-10: 0-595-67912-9 (cloth)
ISBN-10: 0-595-85821-X (ebk)

Printed in the United States of America

This work is dedicated to the thousands of volunteers with whom I've worked. Each has taught me something important about the power of passionate commitment and the significance of personal involvement.

It is also dedicated to my life companion, Pamela Transue, who provides a vibrant example of nonprofit leadership and adherence to principles of absolute integrity and total accountability

Table of Contents

Acknowledgements

It goes without saying that any book that reflects a quarter century of experience in a single profession relies heavily on the wisdom and knowledge of others. Every day since the first moment when I decided to become a capital campaign consultant has been a learning experience. These experiences are brought together in this book, which serves as a tribute to all those from whom I have learned what I know.

My ongoing gratitude to Sonya Campion, my colleague for almost two decades, is boundless. She has set a standard for excellence, helped define best practices in our field, and fought incessantly for the need to systematize our knowledge. She has created many of the most innovative strategies for campaigns and designed the tools that countless organizations have used to reach successful conclusions to challenging campaigns.

Dozens of colleagues at The Collins Group, a firm that I owned and led for 15 years, have provided insights that are contained within this book. Volunteers and executives from more than 400 nonprofit organizations have helped complete my education.

A few people stand out, whom I mention at the risk of leaving out those equally as important in my education. Hank Goldstein and Marilyn Bancel of The Oram Group provide bi-coastal wisdom and common sense. Hank's comment that "retirement is training wheels for death" was one of the inspirations for my working on this book. The late Dave Bixel provided a constant reminder that humor, intelligence, and belief in what can happen combine for success.

Dick Collins, who founded The Collins Group, helped pioneer the concepts that capital campaign consulting is both a calling and a profession and that the only acceptable level of work is that which represents the highest possible professional standards. This book reflects much of his influence, especially in the chapters on preparing for campaigns.

Over the course of hundreds of projects, I worked with thousands of volunteers and learned something from each of them. Helen Peterson, an elder for the Makah Tribe in Neah Bay, Washington, demonstrated that ultimate wisdom lies with volunteers. Tacoma's Bill and Bobby Street and Wendy and Jim Griffin showed me that volunteers can reshape an entire community. Seattle's Matt Griffin helped me understand the potential of the new donors from the high tech sector that has blessed the Northwest. Portland's Milt Carl showed that no goal was too high if a passionate volunteer provided the leadership needed to reach it.

I have had the privilege of working with many skilled fundraising executives and executive directors. Mary Kaufman-Cranney of the Greater Seattle YMCA offered me a decade-long education on how to build donor relations through volunteer activities, while the organization's CEO Neil Nicoll taught me that unflinching adherence to principles of integrity and honesty is always right. Portland State University's Donna Schaeffer demonstrated how long-term commitment to a single organization can pay off in great success. Cindy Zehnder of TVW (Washington's public affairs network) showed that total fearlessness by a CEO can lead an organization to new heights.

Grantmakers and donors helped complete my education. Dr. Buster Alvord, a world-renowned pathologist and a generous patron of the arts, reminded everyone that "After performing more than 30,000 autopsies, I can state with absolute certainty that can't take it with you." Jill Ryan, long-time community affairs manager at SAFECO, has provided ongoing guidance about what foundations are concerned with when they review proposals. Brad Cheney, director of his family's foundation, has provided the ultimate example of a funder whose sole concern is using his foundation's funds to build a stronger community.

Needless to say, while more than 100 people have reviewed and commented on this book over the past months, any shortcomings and errors remain my own. I want to express my gratitude to all those who have helped strengthen and clarify this work, especially my brother Warren Grover, who has provided love and guidance for my entire life, and Pamela Transue, who shares my life and provides me with inspiration, while also embodying the best in nonprofit leadership.

Stuart Grover
September, 2006

Foreword

Standing on the Brink

Ten years ago, you started subscribing to the theatre season, taking your kid to the museum, or volunteering at the local hospital or Boys and Girls Club. Gradually, you began making significant financial donations, expressing opinions about the organization's future, and demonstrating that you considered yourself part of the organization's family.

Then, the organization invited you onto their board. You agreed, because you cared a lot about what the group did. Your commitment continued to deepen. You discovered new ways in which the organization could serve its community and watched with pride as the organization grew and prospered.

And now, the organization needs enlargement and renewal, more space and better facilities. If you don't have enough pews for the congregation, if your waiting list for subscriptions is 200 names long, if your patients have to go elsewhere for basic services, you know it's time to grow and improve.

Your board has started talking about a capital campaign. The activities involved in such a campaign are somewhat disquieting. You'll be expected to give—but how much? You'll be expected to ask people for money—but how? How will you oversee a multi-million construction project? How will the organization pay for studies, know which consultant to hire, and how much to pay?

This book is for you

Over the past 25 years I've consulted with more than 300 organizations and thousands of volunteers in the same position as you. I've heard almost every conceivable question and helped quell most of the concerns people like you have felt.

This book combines my experience with what I've learned from top consultants from throughout North America who've faced the same issues. It's a brief guidebook that will allow you to learn everything you need to know before you take the plunge. A quick read will ensure that you have the confidence and the knowledge to make good decisions and avoid common pitfalls awaiting board members during campaigns.

Get ready to dive in

Most of us remember the first time we stood on the edge of a pier. We knew how to swim, but we'd never swum so far or in water so deep. What if we got a cramp or ran into a snake?

And then we realized that if we could swim in five feet of water, we could swim in 30 feet of water. Unless we dove in, we'd never enjoy that cool, inviting water with our friends.

You're on the edge of the pier. In the distance sits a stronger organization. In between lies a capital campaign that's not much different from what you've been doing as a board member all along. It's been like swimming in the community pool—safe, perhaps fairly shallow, certainly well-supervised.

Now you have the opportunity to swim in deeper waters, where you can have an effect that people in your community (or perhaps region or the entire nation) can enjoy and appreciate for decades or centuries. You can save souls or lives, open minds, or prepare young people for productive lives.

You can swim. Rather than thinking about the hazards of the journey, keep your mind on the goal. You can enjoy the swim and look back upon it as a great adventure. But the reward is the destination, not the journey. You'll always be able to look back upon this campaign and know that you've made a difference in the life of your community.

Introduction

Who this Book Is for
Why Fundraising Is Good and Why It
Needs You if It Is to Succeed

This book carries a single message:

Nothing you do in your life will ever give you more personal satisfaction than leading a successful capital campaign. It will be your chance to be a hero, even if that is the furthest thing from your mind.

Americans, from the start, have looked to ourselves rather than the government to create better communities. Since the initial settlement of our country, citizens have given money and property in response to requests by community leaders.

Charitable gifts and voluntary associations founded our first universities, built the churches that took root on our shores, created homes for the indigent and outcast, and established our first hospitals and homes for the aged. In the early 20th century philanthropy took an activist position, addressing social problems in the belief that private citizens, working through voluntary associations, could do a better, more efficient job than government in correcting social ills. Over the past quarter century, this belief has accelerated.

Professional fundraisers came late to these efforts, only in the early twentieth century. Until recently, it was the men and women of towns and cities who banded together, set goals, and enlisted like-minded people to support their visions. You follow in their footsteps, fundraising amateurs willing to act on behalf of causes you care about.

This book honors the spirit of those pioneers and encourages you to provide volunteer leadership for campaigns. We will create new and better institutions only if <u>individuals</u> renew and expand their commitment to community building. Government entities will commit funds only where they see local support, corporations no longer see it as their responsibility, and foundations look to individuals to guide where they place their money.

This Book Is for Builders

Nonprofit organizations raise two types of money:

- Operating funds, that keep the lights on and pay for salaries and programs
- Money to grow, to support new programs, special projects, expanded or new buildings, and endowment funds for sustainability

This book addresses this second type of money—which usually involves some sort of special campaign and reflects extraordinary requests.

At the core of this book lies a single truth:

> *The vast majority of fundraising campaigns succeed because they attract passionate, committed, skilled volunteer leadership—people like you!*

In thousands of projects people like you have offered leadership with no thought of financial reward. They have represented projects to the community, given generous gifts, and asked others to give, without thought of getting anything back.

Every year, thousands more volunteers serve on boards or committees that support nonprofit organizations. They may be trying to get a community arts center off the ground or supporting a university department that needs a new research space. They may be the board of an opera company whose audience demands a better performance space or of a Girl Scout Council that needs more room for programs.

These needs place volunteer leadership at the center of fundraising efforts. While the fundraising profession has expanded exponentially, nothing replaces the power of volunteers in attracting financial support to worthy projects.

Although more than 90% of all campaigns succeed, no volunteer can approach raising $1 million or more without fear and concern. How can you succeed? Who do you know that will give? How much should you give personally?

This book collects in one place the lessons I have learned from thousands of volunteers who have shared their wealth, enthusiasm, and talent with organizations. You will find here useful advice about your role during a campaign, along with assurance that you can and will succeed.

The Charitable Context

According to the Trust for Philanthropy in their annual compendium "Giving USA," Americans gave away more than $250 billion in 2005, more than $1000 for each adult living in the country. It is also about 1.9% of all money earned in this country, a percentage that has remained relatively stable over the past century.

Such charitable behavior is unequalled anywhere else. Our generosity is the envy of other nations and a source of strength for the United States.

According to the Trust, in any given year between 70 and 80% of all Americans make a cash gift to at least one charity. Surveys reported annually in the *Chronicle of Philanthropy* indicate that more than 90% of all Americans engage in charitable activity every holiday season, whether it be cash gifts, volunteering their time, or purchasing gifts that at least partially benefit a charity.

The less people make, the higher the percentage they give away. Churches get the most money, but people give the biggest gifts to colleges and universities, hospitals, and arts organizations. Millions of people give to social services, environmental groups, humane societies, and international aid organizations.

Most gifts are small—one dollar to $250. The majority of the funds given, however, is in large increments—the gifts of $1 billion and more made by Bill Gates, Joan Kroc, Walter Annenberg, and Ted Turner, and the smaller but still enormous gifts made by thousands of other people. In almost every community, individuals or families make gifts of $100,000 or more to get important projects done.

Each year, thousands of organizations decide that they should buy a building they now lease, expand or renovate their current facilities, or build a new building. Communities decide to create a performing arts center or a Boys and Girls Club. Universities find that they need more funds for scholarships.

These decisions result in fundraising campaigns called capital campaigns if they involve a building or endowment campaigns if they are raising a permanent fund to create income that supports an organization's purpose. Campaigns that combine more than one need are labeled as comprehensive. Campaigns have reached goals exceeding $2 billion, raised over a period of up to seven years.

What sets these campaigns apart is that the organization is re-capitalizing itself, just as a for-profit entity does when it issues stock or sells bonds. You are turning to the community for the additional capital you require to expand your organization's capacity and allow it to do a better job of fulfilling its mission. Just as investors decide on the basis of their financial return, your donors will judge you on the basis of the social benefit that results from the community's investment in your project.

This book will focus on campaigns with goals ranging from $1 million to $100 million. Smaller goals can often be reached without full-fledged campaigns, while larger goals affect only a tiny percentage of organizations. Nonetheless, the approaches outlined here apply to all fundraising and you will benefit by remembering the basic lessons contained in the work no matter what you're raising money for or how much money you are attempting to raise.

Part One:

Before You Ask Anyone for Money

Some Things You Should Know before You Read this Book

1. According to research by the Trust for Philanthropy, most charitable gifts (about 80%) come from living individuals. If you're launching a campaign, don't expect the majority of the money to come from businesses (they give about 5%) or foundations (about 11%).

2. Campaigns are governed by the "Rule of 12." One of the few constants in any campaign is that about half the money comes from a dozen gifts. If you think you're going to raise a million dollars by having 1000 people each give $1000, it probably won't work. By the time you finish this book, you'll believe that statement.

3. The most effective way to raise money is for volunteers to ask people they know for gifts face-to-face. No other method, whether email or telephone or employing a sales staff, raises money as effectively and efficiently.

4. It takes money to raise money. Generally, you should expect to spend from 5% to 15% of the campaign goal to raise money. Large campaigns might cost less as a percentage, but will still cost a lot on an absolute basis. The percentage is usually higher if it's your first campaign, a small campaign, or features parties.

5. Money comes from people your organization already knows and who know you. Don't expect gifts from new donors across the country.

6. Public relations efforts seldom raise money by themselves. Good publicity provides a helpful environment in which to raise money, but donors rarely see a story in the paper and write a big check.

Chapter I

Attitude is Everything, but Reliance on Scientifically-Based Fundraising Techniques Helps

Attitude

To succeed as a volunteer within a campaign, you must maintain a relentlessly upbeat attitude. Once you start thinking a campaign might fail, it will.

At the same time, campaigns don't get done by themselves and their success is not pre-ordained. They require true sacrifice and dedication. Attitude isn't enough without hard work.

Most board or committee members think a campaign will either be very easy or very hard. The ones who see it as easy offer many paths to success:

- "Let's get an article in the paper. Someone's sure to see it and write a big check."
- "We have 250 families in the congregation. Everyone should write a $20,000 check."
- "Bill Gates has a huge foundation. Why wouldn't he give us the money?"
- "A bank will lend us the money and we can pay it off in five or ten years."

Other volunteers see roadblocks at every turn:

- "The economy's in the toilet."
- "The Symphony's big campaign has all the money"

- "Not enough people really know about us."
- "Our group doesn't have the big money that's on the board at the art museum."

Neither the optimists nor the pessimists have it right. The campaign will succeed because of well-organized, hard work towards a compelling vision. There will always be competition, economic challenges, and setbacks. You won't attract money solely through public relations or by dividing up the goal into equal slices. Most campaigns reach goals without much help from billionaires.

Everyone has fears and concerns about fundraising, no matter what their position in the community, their experience, or the merits of the project. Fundraising probably fosters even more fears than public speaking. It connects to our unease in discussing money, our fears of rejection, and our concern about forcing our ideas on others. It's not hard to counteract these fears and to assume attitudes that will assure success.

What are the attitudes that ensure success?

Key attitude #1: Giving is joyful

It's easy to fall into the idea that giving is an imposition—something people do against their will and resent. But you know that isn't true.

Think about it. Think about the times you've given money to something you really cared about—a scholarship fund, the local food bank, or other worthy cause close to your heart.

You felt good about doing something for a cause you felt strongly about. You had expressed your love of humankind and helped redress the balance between justice and injustice.

Every year, community colleges give scholarships to students who are the first in their family to attend college. Often, they have an event that introduces the scholarship donors to the recipients. To see how a gift can change a young person's life gives joy and deep satisfaction.

People give because it expresses their deepest values and desires. The result of a gift is joy to the person who gives.

In modern society, relatively few people have time to volunteer. We lack the skills to educate the young or heal the sick. Our gifts, however, can accomplish those goals. When our money translates into a better world, we feel good.

Key Attitude #2: Fundraising is an ethical and admirable enterprise

Somehow, although we gladly give money, we fear that asking for money is unethical. We think of the boiler room operations and the dinner-time phone calls. We forget that we've happily given to Red Cross or the Girl Scouts. When disasters strike, people's first impulse is to give, whether after the 9/11 attacks, the Asian tsunamis, or Hurricane Katrina. Giving offers a sense that we are all part of a larger effort.

Later on, we'll examine the bases of ethics in fundraising, but for now it is essential that you change your attitude. People who raise money for organizations they believe in are the most ethical, honest people around. Ask the right way and you will never, ever have to compromise your personal ethics.

Key Attitude #3: People who raise money are the luckiest people in the world

Many people think that asking for contributions will lose them friends or alienate them from their community. They fear that people will start crossing the street when they see them coming, seeking to avoid unpleasant encounters.

Fortunately, reality doesn't bear out these fears. Men and women who raise money for community priorities become heroes, setting themselves apart as fearless, selfless, and brave. They do something wonderful—create better communities.

Think of the people who are lionized in your community. In most cases, they have served as chairs of fundraising campaigns. They are the ones "who get things done." They are leaders. They have earned respect because they have been brave enough to stand up for what they believe in.

Campaign leadership is both a mark of respect and a testing ground. People ask you to participate in a campaign because they see in you the skills and traits that others admire. They want to follow your direction. Others see you as embodying credibility and integrity, because those are the characteristics that inspire others.

Key Attitude #4: You're not asking for money for yourself

When you're part of a campaign, it is too easy to equate what you're doing with begging. You're going to your friends to ask for money and you may feel that their gift is to you personally.

In fact, you are serving only as a conduit for the organization, not acting out of self interest. Your friends understand that you are asking them to support a cause you believe in. They listen to you because they respect you, but they'll give because they believe in the mission you're there to talk about. If they say no, it is not because of any lack of respect for you.

When you ask for money on behalf of a cause, you are acting from a desire to do good, not to advance your career or your finances. Before you've asked anyone else for a gift, you've spent dozens of hours learning about and shaping the project. You've also made your own gift to demonstrate your belief. Your request for your friend to join you simply gives him or her the chance to feel joy through supporting a good cause.

Key Attitude #5: No one will do something unless they want to

We all know the feeling. You are about to ask a friend for a gift and you fear that you're going to force them to do something they really don't want to. You're going to use your friendship and their good will to manipulate them into saying yes.

Except that isn't what happens. People in today's world are sophisticated about charitable giving and their own personal priorities. They won't give to something they don't believe in and they will never give more than they can afford. You are serving as a matchmaker, establishing a connection between your friend and a cause he might find joy in supporting. Just as a real-life matchmaker doesn't always succeed in creating a marriage, you won't always find the perfect match. Your friend has free will and you will not lead him or her astray. *On the other hand, they can't give if they're not asked.*

Key Attitude #6: The campaign is going to succeed

If you've ever played golf, you know that a belief in your ability to hit a shot properly is central to your success. If you think you're going to hit the ball into the rough, you probably will. If you are convinced that you'll land it in the middle of the fairway, your chances for a straight drive are better.

Fundraising is no different. If you can focus on your feeling of accomplishment at the campaign's completion and imagine the satisfaction you'll feel at having played a role in the project's success, you will do better than if you contemplate the humiliation you'd feel if you fail. While you should always retain a little nervousness and fear, your primary focus should be on the inevitable success of your efforts.

Your belief has a basis in fact. Whatever the economic climate, whatever the cause, whatever region, more than nine out of ten campaigns succeed. The ones that fail usually reflect extraordinary, but avoidable circumstances.

Communities band together to follow the initiative of those brave enough to lead. Hidden wealth appears, known wealth extends itself to new levels, or new wealth emerges in response to worthy causes. You provide the magic ingredient of leadership that creates a catalytic effect on others.

Final Thoughts on Attitude

With few exceptions, every individual (volunteer or staff) involved in a major campaign starts the process with some fear and concern. All the words staff members and consultants have spoken and written over the past quarter century have not eased those concerns very much, but by the end of their campaigns almost all the people involved held the six key attitudes.

Why?

Because they lived them. They found themselves cast into the role of leader by their friends. They discovered that they were giving others the chance for joy. They discovered that asking for support was fun and strengthened existing relationships. They made new friends. Perhaps most importantly, they found a level of satisfaction in their project's success that they had never expected could exist. Talk to people you know who have been part of successful campaigns. In all probability, they hold these attitudes. After you provide leadership, you will too.

But success also depends on scientifically-proven fundraising methods

Just as other professions have standards and rules, so does fundraising. It has ethical standards (see the next chapter) and methodologies that have been shown to work in peer-reviewed, replicable research.

The approaches suggested in this book reflect both the ethical and scientific bases of fundraising. The three major scientific bases for capital campaigns include:

- Campaigns must be something other than business as usual. Both volunteers and donors receive motivation from a well-organized, focused campaign with a designated start and finish and a clearly-stated goal.

- Campaigns request large sums of community funds. In return for these funds, you must demonstrate the social benefit of the investment you are requesting. The more concrete you can make the outcomes of the campaign, the more likely you are to succeed.

- Donors and volunteers respond to bold and innovative visions. The larger the vision, the more likely your community is to provide an enthusiastic response.

Chapter II

The Ethical Bases of Fundraising

Ethics Are Essential

We all get fundraising calls asking for money for obscure organizations with names that sound vaguely familiar or that invoke respected institutions. These calls from the State Patrol Widows' Fund or the Firefighters Garden Club interrupt our dinners and irritate us. We often find out later that they're scams, with no relationship to the organization whose name they use.

If we've fallen for these pleas, we get mad. If we haven't given money, we probably also get mad and we allow this anger to reflect on our attitudes toward fundraising in general.

We also read about the questionable behavior and improper use of money by a small number of charitable organizations. The head of a national nonprofit used his expense account to finance his relationship with a teenager. Money given to an organization for a specific disaster was put aside to use for future disasters. Can we trust that the money we give or that we ask for will go to the purpose it's meant?

Fundraising often seems to rely on techniques that make us feel uncomfortable. We equate fundraising requests with high pressure sales calls. Even the terminology of fundraising reflects this attitude. How many times do we hear about the need to "put the arm" on a friend, or refer to a charitable request as "hitting up old Joe" for a gift? These phrases and tactics sound and feel unsavory.

Fundraising Does Have a Code of Ethics

The Association of Fundraising Professionals (AFP) has more than 4000 members worldwide. The AFP oversees the most widely accepted professional credential in the field, that of Certified Fundraising Executive (CFRE). Their code of ethics and the accompanying Donor Bill of Rights can be found on their Web site, Afpnet.org. The Giving Institute (formerly the American Association of Fundraising Counsel) also has a code of Standards of Practice for its members, who represent the largest and best known consulting firms in the United States. These codes of ethics provide universally accepted approaches to fundraising that rule out the noxious practices of boiler room efforts and high pressure sales.

Our Personal Ethical Responsibilities

We want to do things that establish us as leaders and demonstrate that we are ethical and honest people. How do we engage in fundraising in a way consistent with those desires?

The answer is simple. We should make sure that our organizations and we, as their representatives, behave in ways that are totally and unarguably ethical. Our actions should reflect three main ethical elements.

Ethical Element I: The donor rules

Donors should give only because they want to, not because they feel obliged to. They should give because it gives them joy and reflects their personal values and desires. Your task is to make certain that the people you ask to support your cause feel good after they give and continue to feel good about their gift.

This simple concept dictates your approach.

- You have to find out what they care about
- They must tell you what appeals to them and what doesn't
- If they don't care about your project, they shouldn't give

Your request must focus on what the money will do rather than what it will build. They won't want to build a museum; they'll want to make art part of everyone's life. They don't want to build a cancer center; they want to eliminate cancer as a cause of human suffering and death.

Ethical Element II: You have to be open and honest about your organization

Those dinner-time phone calls bother you because they're so vague and evasive. They expect you to give without knowing about the organization they represent. When you ask them financial questions, they're usually unwilling to give full information about exactly how the money will be used.

You, on the other hand, will always remain on the ethical high ground. You are not receiving money to ask for the gift and have no financial interest in whether or not your friend gives. Your involvement reflects your own passion for the mission. You're proud of the organization and everything it does.

You'll tell your friend virtually anything she wants to know about the organization, since it's all public information anyway:

- Your organization's financial situation
- How money is used
- The percentages of their gift that go toward the project and for fundraising
- Why the project is important
- Whom it will serve
- Why it will make a difference

You'll answer the questions you can and offer to help them find answers to those questions you can't answer. They will make their decision based on complete information. They will never feel that they're being called upon to purchase a pig in a poke.

Ethical Element III: Your organization should be totally accountable for all money received

After your organization receives a gift, they must communicate with the donor. This begins with a timely acknowledgement of the gift, tax receipts, and other legally-required documentation. It continues with ongoing communication about how the money is being used on the project.

For very large gifts, it might mean a personal tour of the construction site, semi-monthly updates on campaign progress, and other factual and complete information. When the project is over the accountability continues, with a focus on outcomes rather than facilities or endowment.

If a donor has given a gift that includes permanent recognition, they should be invited to see the space or plaque containing their name. If you have a grand opening, they should receive an invitation and tour. As operations start in a new facility, they should receive reports on how the facility allows you to do a better job of fulfilling your mission.

The wonderful part of total accountability is that it offers a reason for you to remain in contact with your donors. They will become part of the organization and feel a sense of close relationship to its people and programs. When it comes time to launch your next campaign, they will be prepared to help you.

The Outcomes of Ethical Fundraising

If you stick to the three elements of ethical fundraising, several of your fears will disappear. Your friends and acquaintances will do something that gives them pleasure, based on complete and honest information. They will receive acknowledgement and recognition for their gifts and be in a position to take pride in the achievements they have made possible.

You will feel certain that your fundraising involved neither coercion nor manipulation. The donors will have engaged in an even-handed relationship in which you have given them the opportunity to fulfill their most deeply held values.

Your organization, through transparency and accountability, will also ensure the proper use of donated funds. You will obey all accounting rules, establish the correct controls over handling of contributions, and be able to show where every dollar went.

Chapter III

How You Know You're Ready for a Campaign

Before your organization can even think about raising money, they should:

- Have a strategic plan.
- State their vision.
- Decide who it will benefit and how.
- Describe how they will sustain it in the future.
- Define the project scope and cost and demonstrate the ability to manage the scope and cost.

These are the steps to figuring out what you're raising money to do. In general, you should define your project within 15% of your final outcome if you hope to get anyone beyond your board and staff interested in it.

A project is more complex than building something or creating an endowment. It has to start with a strategic plan and a vision.

The Strategic Plan

Your organization needs to know where it wants to go and what it wants to do. It has to have clearly defined, concrete goals and objectives and possess the strategies needed to achieve them. All other elements of a campaign must emanate from this strategic plan.

What's a Vision?

A vision for a nonprofit should always focus on what you could do for the community if you had the money you needed. Seattle's Fred Hutchinson Cancer

Research Center has a vision of "eradicating cancer as a cause of human suffering and death." When gifts build a new laboratory, support a researcher, or create an endowment, donors help move the Hutch closer to achieving its vision.

Visions are different than mission statements, because they are more daring, more ambitious, and go beyond who you are and how you spend your time now. They reach into the future to describe what can happen if enough people share your vision.

Organizations can sometimes renew their visions. A small adoption agency had long held a vision of "helping unite families with the children who need them." As the 20th century unfolded, they understood that the needs of children had become more complex and that adoption was not always the best or only answer. They created a new vision of "serving as the voice for children in need." This required them to grow, to offer new services, and to redefine their mission. They did these things, becoming a leader in the field of children's issues.

Assessing the Need for Your Services

Once your organization has either developed a new vision or confirmed the old one, it's time to relate this vision to your future. The first step is to test your vision against the reality of the marketplace for your services.

- If your nonprofit theatre company operates in a leased 120-seat theatre, is there enough demand to warrant purchasing your own building with a 200-seat capacity? You don't want to make a dreadful mistake that changes the nature of your company and leaves you with empty seats and a gaping hole in your budget.

- A skilled nursing home that served severely disabled children operated in an old and tired building. They wanted to build a better facility, but needed to know whether the number of children needing long-term care would remain at its current level, increase, or decline. Interviews with physicians, insurers, and others determined that the number of such children was likely to decline—but the need for *short term* care of medically fragile children would grow. The nursing home was positioned to serve parents who needed respite care for their children or whose children needed short-term care. The nursing home built a new facility to meet both old and new needs and now serves almost three times the families it did before, although with the same number of beds.

- A hospital system wanted to build a new facility in a small town nine miles away from its largest hospital. Would local residents use the new hospital or would they prefer to stay with current facilities they used, belonging either to the system or its major competitor? A needs assessment established that the community wanted its own hospital.

Establishing the need for your facility, through objective, professional research allows your board members to give their own money and ask others for gifts with the assuredness that the money will go to good use. It also ensures that you are living up to the responsibilities of maintaining your tax-exempt status that requires fulfilling a community benefit.

Showing That Your Project Is Sustainable

The needs assessment serves as the basis for a business plan.

Just because a nonprofit doesn't pay dividends to its owners, it should still generate a surplus. A nonprofit is a business that has to generate enough revenue to pay for its operations (through both earned income and contributed funds).

A surplus can provide cash reserves, serve as an internal line of credit, provide money to buy new equipment or maintain your building, or allow you to expand your services.

Organizations need to demonstrate that their future revenue will be sufficient to support their new operations. No one wants to contribute to a new building only to see the organization go bankrupt a year or two later. When an organization fails after a capital campaign, the effect on future operations is catastrophic. Equally as important, such a failure makes donors lose faith in the entire nonprofit sector.

A conservative, carefully done business plan reassures donors (and the board) that you know what you're getting into. It provides hard numbers based on transparent assumptions. How many people have to visit your museum for you to break even? How soon does your nursing home have to achieve 80% capacity for you to stay in business?

You have to know who your competitors are, what potential pitfalls you face, and know enough about your line of business to forecast your future. Consultants can help you in this process, but it is the board's responsibility to review the plan carefully and ensure that its assumptions are realistic.

- An ethnic cultural center received a business plan that assumed that 1% of all car traffic going through the community would stop to visit, translating into a potential 250,000 visitors. No other cultural facility in the community drew more than 50,000 people. Yet the board chose to believe the business plan's projections and borrowed money to purchase a building. Attendance barely reached 10,000 the first year and the center had to sell the building and give up their dream.

Several inexpensive computer-generated business plans work extremely well as outlines for nonprofit organizations planning new or expanded facilities. They remind organizations of all the factors that influence the bottom line. If you've performed an accurate needs assessment and have board members with a strong business background, there's no reason why you can't create your own business plan. The challenge is always the same. A business plan is only as good as the honesty and hard-headedness of the assumptions on which it's based.

Defining the Project

Defining a physical project precisely will help you raise money and strengthen your organization. Never forget that the building (or endowment) is only a vehicle for helping you achieve your mission and vision.

People won't give money for a new hospital or an endowment. They'll give money to guarantee "quality care close to home," or "leveling the playing field through scholarships."

You have to express your building or endowment goals through mission/vision-based outcomes. The Kresge Foundation, one of America's most respected charitable foundations, describes the process as an hourglass. You pass the organization's current strength through the hourglass to get to the future vision at the bottom of the hourglass.

For example, *"The addition to the YMCA will let us provide 450 more at-risk youth with after-school activities."*

or

"A $3 million scholarship endowment will let 30 students annually be the first in their family to attend college."

or

"Forty million dollars for a new performance hall will bring world-class musicians to our region for the first time and reinvigorate our downtown core."

That's the big picture. But you also have to get into details. This is called the "building program" and it's where the hard work comes:

- What activities will occur in the building and how much room will be used for each separate activity?

- How will the flow of the building work? If you're building a new animal shelter, how will the building minimize the stress on lost, scared pets and frantic pet owners, ensuring that pets will stay healthy and happy while waiting to be claimed?

- If you're enlarging your independent school, what types of rooms and assembly spaces will you need?

More specialized buildings are even more complex and the program will take longer to develop.

Ideally, a program will demonstrate what will occur in the new facility, how the flow of activities will proceed, and why your investment will yield important outcomes. When you're creating the building program, imagine how you will tell the prospect why the new space is an improvement on the old, whether in terms of numbers of people served, level of service, or efficiency of service. For example, if you're creating the program for a cancer treatment center, think how effective it would be to say:

The new reception area affords privacy to the patient, ensuring that they can provide private details without sharing them with other clients. The area will also be attractive and comfortable, and provide a soothing environment at a stressful time.

The Functional Program Doesn't Need Pretty Pictures

Organizations are always in a hurry to produce architectural plans with attractive views (renderings) of the finished product. Don't succumb to the temptation.

Architectural plans go through many phases, starting with programming what spaces will be needed and how the spaces will relate to each other. This is all you need to start.

We recommend against having the architect prepare schematic drawings at this point. Such plans can cost tens of thousands of dollars or more. This money will be wasted, since either you'll decide not to move ahead with the project at all or to move ahead with a much altered project.

To show possible donors a rendering at this point is a problem, since they will expect a finished product to look like what they saw. If it doesn't, they'll accuse you of a "bait and switch."

To judge your project, potential supporters need to know what you're planning to do, how much space it will take, and how much it will cost—all within a factor of about 15% of where you wind up. People understand that you can't know everything at the start and also appreciate that you're asking their advice before you make your plans final. Functional programs reflect the mission and vision in a direct, easily explainable way and avoid having people get fixated on design.

The functional program also gives you lots of flexibility, because there are many ways to provide various types of space. You can have separate classrooms and meeting space, or a single space that combines both functions. Even if you can raise less money, you can fulfill the functional program to everyone's satisfaction. If you show people a seemingly finished product with two classrooms and a large meeting hall, that's what they'll remember and expect. Having a single large room that can be divided in two will seem like a big change, because they'll be focused on the physical rather than the programmatic element.

Chapter IV

Testing Your Dream

Why a Feasibility Study?

"Everyone I've talked to thinks this is a great idea. Why waste money having a consultant talk to the same people?"

That's what you're probably thinking when someone on your board suggests doing a feasibility study. You've been out in the community talking up the new performing arts center and you haven't heard one word against it. You just know that fundraising the $5 million or $15 million or $100 million you need to make it a reality will be a slam dunk.

Or do you?

Have you heard definitively from anyone that they'll make the $3 million gift necessary to get the project off the ground?

Has anyone talked to the small theatre companies that now receive free performance space in a church to see if their donors will support your project?

Do you know what the most effective way to present the project to the community will be? Are they interested in it as an economic generator for downtown? As a place to expose youths to art? As a home to local musical groups?

Who are the people willing to go out and ask for the money and make speeches to Rotary and Kiwanis about the project?

These are all things that a professionally-run study can tell you. A good study can help you avoid embarrassment and make sure you organize your efforts most effectively.

Choosing a Consultant

No matter where you live, someone locally or regionally says they can do a study cheaply and accurately. Maybe they can. But before you hire the insurance guy's handball partner, there are some things to think about.

- Do you feel comfortable entrusting your project to this person? Is he or she the type of person you want representing your project to the broader community. Do you believe they'll tell you the truth, even if it means telling you things you don't want to hear?

- Has he or she done at least ten studies, including several on projects somewhat similar to yours in terms of size or focus?

- Does the consultant belong to regional and national organizations and possess appropriate credentials? The Giving Institute is the gold standard of the profession, but membership in the Association of Fundraising Professionals (AFP) and accomplishment of the Certificate of Fundraising Executive credential (CFRE) are good signs as well. Do a Web search on them, and see whether they've made speeches, written articles, and won acclamation in the field.

- Do they have strong references? Call four or five of their past clients— not just the ones they suggest.

- Are they trying to sell you a package deal, asking you to agree to both the study and following campaign management? Such a package means they have an interest in showing a campaign is feasible, lessening your chances of an objective study.

- Is the person 'selling' the contract the same one who will be carrying it out?

- *Most importantly,* does the consultant seem to actually know and care about your project? Have they done research on your organization? If they haven't thought about you when they're trying to get your business, will it get better after they have your account?

How to Find a Consultant

First off, don't start by putting out a general request for proposals (RFP). It's not fair to you or to the consultant.

Establish a small committee to retain the consultant. Their process should include the following:

- Call up six to eight nonprofits in your region who have recently done capital campaigns and get recommendations

- Go on the web and check to see if there's a Giving Institute consultant in your area.

- Look in the Yellow Pages and see if there are any specialized consultants in your area.

- Contact half a dozen or so consultants or firms and request that they send you their qualifications

- After review, develop a short list of two to four firms that seem to be a good fit for you

- Once you have that short list, prepare a brief rfp to explain your project, talk about your organization, and explain what you hope to find out from a study.

You'll notice that I haven't mentioned cost yet. Fit is a much more important criterion. The least expensive consultant is seldom the best choice, but neither is the most expensive. If you absolutely can't spend more than $37,500, it's not fair to hide that and then disqualify or penalize proposals for more than that amount. You should also provide a timeframe. If you need the study within a set time, let the consultant know. Studies take from a month to four or five to complete, depending on the size and complexity of the project.

Most good studies take at least three or four months. Don't shortchange yourself by thinking you need an answer tomorrow. Most projects suffer when rushed.

Assign one person to answer consultant questions. Nothing's worse for a consultant than to guess at your intent or interest.

Give the consultants at least two weeks to respond. Then, review the proposals and get back to them within a week or ten days. If all the proposals are responsive and personalized, interview all the candidates. If two stand out, then only interview those.

The committee should spend at least an hour with each finalist. All committee members should be present at all interviews. You may be able to get it done in a day or you may have to spread the interviews over a week.

Make clear that you want the candidates to present for no more than half the time and leave the rest for give and take. Prepare questions beforehand and ask at least some of the same questions of each group. If you have specific questions about a specific proposal, ask. If one of the finalists quotes a very high or very low price, request an explanation. Remember that $10,000 represents a very small part of your entire project

Make your choice and ask for a contract. Make certain that there were no hidden costs or surprises, that the consultant they promised will perform the work, and that they can get it done within the timeframe you need.

How Much Should a Study Cost?

Not surprisingly, costs vary widely for studies. Firms that work nationally charge anywhere from $15,000 to $100,000 for studies, depending on the size of the project and the number of people they will be contacting. For most projects that are trying to raise between $2 million and $20 million, you should be able to get a good study for under $50,000. You'll probably get bids well under that and perhaps some above that level. Your decision should focus on the product you want and the 'feel' you get for the consultant.

Variables that will affect the cost of the study include:

- Does it include an assessment of your current fundraising? If you have a large department (or even two or three people), such an assessment might add $10,000 or more to the cost

- Who is preparing the materials describing the project? If the consultant is responsible for writing, designing, and printing the 'case statement,' it often involves $5,000 or more. If they're skilled at such activities, it's well worth it.

- How many interviews are they doing? Make sure they're doing enough to get a good cross section of information. You can often save money by offering to schedule the interviews at a central location to save travel time.

- Are they charging you to travel to your site? Out-of-town firms will generally charge you for plane fare and hotels. If they have to make half a dozen trips, this can add up, especially if you're not on an airline 'hub.' Encourage them to consolidate travel to lower costs.

- Are they doing focus groups or doing a mail or email survey? These will also add costs but provide valuable information.

- How many people are they assigning to the study? More people cost more, but provide a more balanced view.

- How detailed a report will they present to you? A brief report takes less time to write and may contain the basic information you think you need. A more detailed report may get read by only a few people, but contains the nuances that will help shape a successful campaign.

The cost of the study is less important than the trust you feel for its conclusions. A cheap study is wasted money if you don't have the information you need or can't trust the information it presents. An expensive study that provides trustworthy and detailed information can shorten the campaign, make it more successful, and save you hundreds of thousands of dollars in fundraising and financing costs.

How Can You Pay for a Study?

Organizations pay for studies in one of three ways:

- They use cash reserves they have amassed for precisely the purpose of launching a campaign. These funds are helpful to pay for all of the work suggested in the two previous chapters—a needs assessment, architectural work on the functional program, and the feasibility study

- A generous patron or patrons might provide the funds either as a gift or as a forgivable loan that doesn't have to be repaid if the campaign doesn't move forward. Some local foundations are willing to provide this type of grant and some organizations have 'angels' who will invest in the organization's future.

- The organization's board members may put up the initial funds to get the project off the ground.

You should be aware that these studies are part of the capitalization of the project and should eventually be charged to the campaign. The expenses will show up on your balance sheet rather than on your profit and loss statement.

Chapter V

Does Anyone Care?
The Feasibility Study

What Happens During a Study?

Once you've hired a consultant, they will ask to review information about your organization and the project. Usually, they'll want to work with a small committee to provide guidance and make certain they're answering the questions you need them to address.

They'll need your help in three aspects of the study:

- How to describe the project
- What issues you want to find answers for
- Who they should talk with

The Case Statement

Whether you or the consultant writes the case statement, the document has to be carefully prepared. It should be brief enough to be read within five minutes and establish how the community will benefit from your project.

A good case statement will provide a strong sense of what will happen to those the project touches. It will explain how a new hospital will change a community's health care or how an expanded museum will provide new educational opportunities for children. It will offer clear information about the project budget and describe how you will sustain the organization in the future.

Depending on the project and your community, the case statement can be simple or ornate, a few pages of word-processed text or a full-color brochure. It can be on your organization's letterhead or on heavy, glossy stock that oozes expense. It doesn't work for a small social service organization to create a glossy brochure to describe a $1 million expansion project for addicted teens. On the other hand, museum supporters would be disappointed to be mailed a few sheets of copy paper describing a $75 million expansion.

Defining Critical Issues

One overarching concern defines all feasibility studies:

> *Do enough people care about your project to provide the money needed to get it done?*

That is always the bottom line in every study, but many separate issues make up that ultimate determination. These include six categories of concerns.

I.   Your organization

- Is your organization the right one to take on this challenge or should it be cooperating with others?

- Do people have confidence in your organization?

- Is your organization strong enough to take on new challenges?

II.   Availability of leaders

- Is your board respected and seen as up to the task?

- Is your chief executive seen as an effective leader?

- Will other respected community leaders step up to provide leadership for the campaign?

- Is there an obvious candidate for campaign chair?

III. Case for support

- What does the community see as the most important benefit of your project?

- Will your project make a significant difference to the community's well-being?

- Do your projected outcomes (people served, changes made) strike people as worth the amount of money you're raising?

IV. Giving Potential

- Will people give and how much?

- Will the people you count on the most give the size of gifts you're hoping they will?

- How far away from your core group can you go and still hope to get large gifts?

- Will local and regional foundations and corporations make gifts?

V. Are you ready?

- To raise money, you need staff, software, hardware, and systems. Where does your organization stand in regards to these needs?

- Is the board prepared to be part of a campaign, or do they think it can happen without them?

VI. Is this the right time to start a campaign?

- Are people optimistic enough about the economy and the direction of their lives that they'll make big charitable gifts to you?

- Are there competing campaigns that mean that you should put off your campaign?

If the answers to these questions are mostly positive, you can launch a campaign; if they're mostly negative, you should reconsider. Feasibility studies provide accurate information if they're done by competent, experienced consultants. They either find potential gifts or they don't. The community either tells them you're a strong, deserving organization or they mutter a collective "Huh?" The study either identifies strong leadership or it doesn't.

Your job as a board member is to make sure the consultant asks the right questions and talks to the right people. Is there something unusual about your project? Are there people that you ordinarily wouldn't consider as major donors who might be motivated to support you?

It's your job to help the study be successful.

Who Should Be Interviewed?

Potential leaders

Potential donors

Opinion makers

Potential bottlenecks

You Can't Talk to Everyone; This Isn't a Marketing Survey

You want to talk to people who can make big gifts—identifying those dozen or so gifts that can guarantee the success of the campaign. You want to identify your leaders. And you want to learn what pitfalls might await you.

Generally, between 35 and 60 people will provide you with all the information you need. If you're a small community and trying to raise $3 million for a new aquatics center or skating rink, 35 people will give the information you need. If you're a private university with 20,000 alums and 1500 students, you'll probably need at least 60 interviews and may choose to do many more.

Why so few? Because you are consciously seeking an elite group of people—the few people who can determine success or failure. No mater how large the campaign or how big your organization, 12 or fewer gifts will make up 50% of your goal. *If you can't identify the 35 to 50 people with the likelihood of making those gifts, you're not ready to do a study.*

For certain projects, you'll also want to use focus groups to broaden your outreach and involve more people in ownership of the project. Independent schools will want to have such structured discussions with groups of teachers, parents, and alumni/ae, as well as holding individual discussions with representatives of its various constituencies.

Leaders

This book began by telling you that leadership is the most important element in the success of fundraising campaigns. So it's no surprise that the first priority of a study is to locate your campaign leadership.

Review your membership, your donor list, your subscriber list, your alumni/ae list. Are there any people whose participation would ensure your success? A museum discovered that the president of a huge international company was a supporter, hailed from the museum's city, and that his wife was close friends with a key volunteer. The feasibility study interview revealed that the couple would be willing to serve as campaign leaders.

Look for logical connections and reasonable expectations. Even if a tycoon gives you $10,000 annually, it doesn't mean he has the time to be part of your campaign—or even that you're a major priority for him.

Donors

Talk to the people who are already your major donors. Anyone who provides 1% or more of your annual fund should be interviewed. You should look carefully at those donors who've given money for many consecutive years or who are among your top ten cumulative donors.

Talk to corporations and foundations that already know about you and that have provided occasional support. There might be regional or national foundations that you should talk to, but make sure they have a logical reason for supporting you.

Make certain you talk to a few current non-donors who give to similar organizations. You want to know why they don't give to you and whether your campaign might appeal to them. A feasibility study interview is a great way to begin developing a relationship with new donors.

Opinion Leaders

Think about who sets the tone in your community. Whose participation and/or support seem to be part of everything important that happens? You'll want to know whether they're on your side or not, and why. While interviews are normally confidential, opinion leaders frequently preface their comments with "I want your board to know that...." The interviewer, after clarifying that the opinion leader is serious, is entitled to carry these thoughts back to you.

Spoilers

Some people love to spoil other people's plans. They glory in being power brokers with the capacity to "make or break" a project. It's important to let them talk to you first, both to give you a clearer view of where they stand and to ensure that they feel part of the process.

Ask around town to find out who's gossiping about the project and leading backroom bickering about it. That's the person you have to talk to before he or she poisons the community.

What Will Happen During the Study?

From your point of view, not much. The consultant contacts people and arranges interviews. Usually, this will instigate some talk throughout the community's inner circles, since it's the first public word about your plans.

Sometimes your friends will stop you on the street and ask you "Why aren't I being interviewed?" If you realize that they should be part of the study, inform the consultant. If not, just say, "Well, we had a limited budget and we can't talk to everyone, unfortunately." Ask them whether they'd like to be informed about the study results and make sure you follow up.

Otherwise, for a period of four to twelve weeks, you'll only receive occasional reports on how the study process is going—if there are any difficulties in getting interviews or whether people are anxious to talk. The consultant may ask for your help in securing interviews with key people. They may ask you for additional background information on interviewees.

What Will the Study Tell You?

A well-conducted study will tell you the most important things you need to know:

- Who will step forward as a leader and what leadership structure will work best
- How much money you can raise and who your big donors may be
- What the most attractive, exciting aspects of your project are and what pieces of the project are detrimental to your success

- How people regard your organization
- What competition or roadblocks you face
- What internal preparation you need before you can launch a campaign and what staff and resources you need to add before starting
- How soon, if at all, you can start your campaign

The consultant will meet with the committee overseeing the study and then with the entire board. It's imperative that all board members read the completed study carefully and that the meeting with the consultant allows enough time to get all questions addressed.

Make certain you understand how the consultants reached the study's conclusions and be certain they can defend them. Now is the time to get your questions answered—if you wait until after the campaign has started to second-guess the study conclusions, it's too late.

Once you've reviewed and discussed the study, you're ready for the next step—confirming your support for an actual campaign.

Chapter VI

We Are Resolved...

So...

The study is complete. You and your fellow board members have heard the results, discussed them, and have reached a crossroad.

Should we proceed?

In almost 200 studies I've been involved with, we recommended moving forward about 75% of the time, although in most cases we suggested spending a few months to a year to prepare for the campaign. In 25% of the cases, we bring back findings that are so negative we cannot suggest any way to move forward with a campaign. While there may be other solutions for the organization, the potential for a successful fundraising campaign is too small to merit the risk.

But let's say you've received positive news and the consultant has recommended that you move forward. You have some potential leaders and donors. The community likes the project and ranks it as a high priority. They agree that your organization has the ability to achieve your goals. No major roadblocks to a successful campaign have emerged.

But you've also heard that although you need $10 million for the proposed building, the consultant thinks you can only raise $8 million. The consultant has also discovered that your top choices for leadership are unwilling to chair the campaign, although they're willing to participate at some level. Your development department is not ready for a campaign without additional staff. And another organization in town plans to announce a $5 million campaign within the next month.

What should you do?

Establish a date by which the board will make a decision, assuming that you are not ready to make one now. Give yourself a few weeks to answer the basic questions that will allow you to decide whether to move forward:

- Can you build a worthwhile project for $8 million?
- If you can't, can you finance the remaining $2 million without compromising future operations?
- Will your ideal leaders help assure success, making a few key calls and serving as spokespeople, even if they won't serve as chairs?
- Is the board willing to support expansion of the development staff?
- Will the other campaign provide competition for major donors? Will anything be gained by waiting?

The board must accept the decision meeting as a major priority. They should schedule it to maximize attendance and set aside enough time to permit full discussion.

The consultant, board chair, and executive director should present a united front, offering their opinions concerning the questions raised during the study. They should fully explain their conclusions and then open the floor for discussion.

The consultant may believe that it's premature for a campaign. He or she might recommend strengthening your board or more fully defining the project. There might be a recommendation to cut back the project or wait until you've gotten a firm commitment for a lead gift. In these cases, the board chair should appoint a committee to address outstanding issues, with time limits to bring solutions back to the board.

If they have recommended moving forward, they should bring with them a formal resolution of support, distributed after their presentation. That resolution should become the basis for discussion once a motion is introduced to pass it.

A sample resolution might read as follows:

"Whereas, the Tuna Falls Community Theatre has provided high quality professional presentations to Tuna Falls and the surrounding area for the past 32 years, and

Whereas, the Theatre has grown in popularity to the point where we have a large waiting list for subscriptions, and

Whereas, our current facility does not permit us to stage productions with more than four characters or requiring live music, and

Whereas, the community has repeatedly expressed the desire for more ambitious, varied theatrical productions, and

Whereas, research has indicated there is a market for renting the theatre during our "dark" period, and

Whereas, we are confident that an expanded theatre with additional seating capacity, fly space, an orchestra pit, and a larger stage will be self-supporting with minimal additional contributed income,

Therefore, we the Board of Directors of the Tuna Falls Community Theatre do solemnly resolve to:

- *Raise a minimum of $8 million to expand and improve our current theatre*
- *Support the fundraising effort enthusiastically and without reserve, including making our own significant gifts*
- *Represent the Theatre and the campaign to our friends and neighbors in the most positive possible fashion, and*
- *Not be satisfied until we have successfully completed these efforts*

Unanimously agreed to, on the ___th day of _____, 2——

(signed)

After you discuss the resolution, take a vote to ensure that everyone agrees. If the resolution doesn't pass unanimously, continue discussions. Once the resolution is signed, it's final and all board members are bound by its provisions. All board members must agree to make a gift that is significant to them. The resolution is a public affirmation of the board's commitment and will be shared with potential donors.

It is possible that you cannot achieve unanimity. It is far better to have one or two board members leave if they cannot support the campaign than to have them fighting a rear-guard action for the next several years.

In almost all cases, however, the board will reach agreement and all members will sign the resolution with enthusiasm and excitement. It represents a major commitment that should be taken with immense seriousness, but is also a cause for celebration. A glass of Champagne or beer, a small party, or other event should mark the decision.

A capital campaign strains every sinew of an organization. If the basic fabric of the organization held together by the board is not strong, the entire enterprise can dissolve quickly. Debate and discussion before you start, no matter how painful, will help create the strongest possible fabric that can withstand any possible tension during the campaign.

Chapter VII

Putting Campaign Central in Place

Why You Need a War Chest

As a board member, you're responsible for setting the campaign budget. This chapter gives you the background to understand why campaigns are expensive.

It is always tempting to think you can raise money without spending very much. After all, you're aware that you're the one who'll be asking for gifts. The executive director gets the same salary as always, although she'll be doing a lot of work on the campaign. You already have a development officer and support staff. You can get a couple of extra computers from the local bank and jury-rig something to handle the campaign data base.

Wrong.

Campaigns require skilled, specialized staff members and consultants in addition to your current staff. You need top of the line computers and specialized software. You will save money in the long run if you have a high quality color printer.

Saving money will cost you money. Fewer staff will mean longer, less successful campaigns. It will also reduce your ability to develop and sustain donor relationships that guarantee your long-term, viability.

It'll take several months after the campaign starts before money starts coming in. You need a war chest to pay salaries, buy equipment, and create campaign materials.

Campaigns Are Labor Intensive

Raising money is about relationships between people. It requires people who are part of your organization to communicate with potential leaders, donors, vendors, and other prospective participants. You must keep close track of all of these relationships, record past meetings' outcomes, schedule current meetings, and plan future meetings. Campaigns operate as continuums, not as an isolated series of events. You must keep accurate, detailed records of all campaign activities.

Managing these relationships and records is the responsibility of "Campaign Central," the nerve center of the campaign, composed of paid campaign staff and consultants whose sole job is to ensure the campaign's success. To raise $1 million or more requires at least one full-time staff person dedicated to the campaign. You will also probably require some level of fund raising consulting and perhaps additional clerical help.

Larger campaigns require more staff. If your campaign is $5 million or more, you will probably need an additional staff person whose primary job is to establish and develop relationships with foundations and corporations, including writing grant proposals. You will also probably require an additional full-time clerical person to handle the increased volume of activity and ensure that no potential donor slips through the cracks. As the size of the goal increases, so does the complexity of the campaign. You may need a part- or full-time public relations officer to coordinate publicity efforts or an additional person to work with committees that focus on smaller gifts. You will probably also need the capacity to do research on potential donors.

Campaign Costs

At the back of this book, you will find a grid that allows you to estimate the cost of running a campaign. Generally speaking, it is difficult if not impossible to run a campaign for less than 5% of the goal, no matter how much you are raising. This percentage rises for smaller campaigns, although the absolute numbers will be much smaller.

First time campaigns are generally the most expensive, because you are starting from scratch in building both systems and relationships. You will have to provide enough staff to do research, arrange meetings, enter data, and perform all the other campaign functions. These start-up costs are proportionally less when you've done a campaign within the last five years.

Campaigns in small towns are often less expensive than those in large cities. There are fewer prospects and fewer media outlets to influence. You have access to leaders and donors without convoluted strategies. Staff costs are often lower as well, since the cost of living is lower.

The Campaign Manager

At the heart of every successful campaign stands a competent, committed, energetic campaign manager, who keeps the campaign moving forward, ensures that volunteers perform properly, and always has his or her finger on the pulse of the campaign. An ideal manager has at least three years' experience as a professional fundraiser, has participated in a campaign, and has top rate professional skills and demeanor. They can be a current employee of the organization or an outside person.

Depending on the size of the organization and the magnitude of the campaign, you will pay a campaign manager between $50,000 and $150,000. If several organizations in a city are undertaking major campaigns, they can get into a bidding war that raises salaries beyond these levels. Salaries and benefits are all legitimately included in the overall campaign goal. The term of employment is ordinarily for the duration of the campaign plus at least another six months to launch an effective stewardship plan.

The Campaign Assistant

If a campaign exceeds about $5 million, the quantity of data that you will be entering exceeds the ability of current staff to oversee it. Lists of prospective donors and leaders, donor lists, gift acknowledgements, donor records, and all the other detail work must be handled with absolute accuracy and great tact. A good campaign assistant will make the work of your committees much more efficient and successful. Depending on the skill and experience level of the campaign assistant, salaries can vary from $20,000 to $45,000.

Qualifications start with two vital characteristics—excellent computer skills and attention to detail. The campaign assistant handles specialized fundraising software, word processing, spread sheets, and desk-top publishing software. They must keep perfect track of a myriad of details and be able to provide required information instantaneously. Campaigns flounder if they rely on inaccurate or insufficient information.

Campaign Consultants

Most campaigns benefit from hiring professional campaign counsel. In most cases, consultants don't take the place of staff, although for smaller campaigns they might.

Consultants are most important to help organize the campaign, provide strategic guidance as the campaign progresses, and offer evaluation of the campaign at each step along the way. They help train your volunteers, provide a constantly-reviewed campaign plan, and offer ongoing reassurance that you're making satisfactory progress toward success.

Working with a consultant who's "been there, done that" lets you profit from past experience and ensures that you follow the most appropriate and effective path to success. The consultant offers a dispassionate outside voice reminding you of best practices and assuring you that you're making correct decisions. He or she provides ongoing oversight of the campaign and prevents you from embarking on fruitless detours. They can explain to the over-enthusiastic volunteer why things are done in a specific way. A good consultant discourages fruitless events, chasing after "other people's money" rather than focusing on donors connected to the project, and ensures that you ask for "no gift before its time."

If you've been happy with the consultant who did your feasibility study, your discussions should start with him or her. Get a bid on how much the campaign will cost, including both fees and expenses. Gain an understanding of precisely what the consultant proposes to do in exchange for the fee. How often will you see her? Will he write grants or will you have to hire an additional person? Will he help you hire your campaign manager and assistant? Does their company have the capacity to help create campaign materials or will you have to retain another company for that purpose?

Consultant Fees

It is unethical and against the canons of professional fundraising for a consultant to be paid on a percentage or contingent basis. There are many reasons for this, but the primary one is that campaigns must reflect shared risk—the organization and the consultant must have skin in the game for a campaign to have the best chance to work. If the onus is on the consultant and they won't get paid unless funds are raised, the nonprofit's volunteers are likely to sit back, rather than participating wholeheartedly in the campaign.

Percentage-based fundraising is also unethical because it appears to create a situation where a portion of the gift goes directly to the consultant. Although sophisticated donors understand that there is a real cost to raising money, they bridle at the thought that a consultant is seeking a gift largely to line his or her own pockets.

Finally, percentage-based fundraising has been abused in the past when consultants pursued easy, large gifts to collect their fees at the start of the campaign and then walked away during the vital, but more difficult portions of the campaign.

Ethical fundraisers usually set their professional fees on the basis of the number of days per month they plan to spend working on the project. Fees vary, but generally reflect experience and success rates. Generally speaking, you should choose a model that fits your true needs, rather than conforming to a pre-conceived budget.

If your campaign is complex and will require many committees and extensive work with funders over a large region, you should retain a consultant with experience in such campaigns. If you're a church with 300 families in the congregation, you might want to have a consultant live in the community for three to six months and organize the campaign on a full-time basis.

The amount you pay your consultant will depend on how you've structured the campaign. If you have many staff members working on the campaign, your consultant will focus on providing strategic counsel. If you're a small agency with a single capital campaign staff member, the consultant will spend much more time on the campaign, performing many campaign-related tasks rather than just "consulting."

In all cases, you should look at total campaign costs. If you're doing a campaign with a $10 million goal, your fundraising costs should probably not exceed $1.2 million. If your consultant suggests a fee that, when added to staff costs and materials, escalates that cost to $1.5 million, the fee is probably too large and involves unnecessary services and expenses.

Hardware

Ten years ago, hardware was a major issue for nonprofits, because computers were relatively expensive and expertise in them was at a premium. Today, that is no longer a problem.

Buy from a reputable dealer, get more capacity than you'll ever think you need, get the bells and whistles, more RAM and disk space than you can imagine—and you'll still not be spending very much. You'll also probably find that in three years, it'll be time to upgrade.

For not much more than $2,000, you can get a top of the line machine that can hold all of your programs, store all your data, communicate with the rest of the world, burn CDs and DVDs, and do all of it fast enough to satisfy the most type-A person.

Avoid any temptation to accept gifts of used computers from local businesses. If they're not good enough for them, they're not good enough for you. Get new, state of the art computers. It's good for morale and good for efficiency. Consider adding a high speed color printer/copier. You'll probably spend less in the long run and save the time spent running to a copy center.

Contact Management Software

Many medium and large-size nonprofits already possess contact management software sufficiently sophisticated to manage a capital campaign. But many do not, relying either on paper records or some form of generic data base such as Excel. While this may be sufficient for annual fundraising, it will not work for a capital campaign involving more than several dozen potential donors.

You will need some form of easily manipulated Contact Management Software. Such software allows you to keep track of your prospects and volunteers, usually along with members, subscribers, and any other supporters. More sophisticated programs will permit you to generate correspondence, check changes of address over the Internet, and even do limited prospect research. Some programs are designed specifically to integrate all financial functions of your organization, so that you can cross reference between donors, members, subscribers, attendees, vendors, and anyone else associated with you.

The only real technical parameters you need to concern yourself with are the number of records you plan to manage. For small organizations, you can use a contact management system available over the Internet. If you have a larger data base, you will want to have an in-house system that allows you to have full control over your records. You will also probably want to have access available from multiple computers or work stations.

Whatever system you use, it must allow you to track all "touches" between the organization and its prospective donors. You will have to generate lists of donors by category and according to the volunteer who has received the assignment to work with them. You will need a field in which you can record notes on each transaction and another to provide ticklers for future actions.

Good software programs are easy to use, produce reports that are highly legible and easy to understand, and can be updated as they improve. They also should come with appropriate technical support. Talk with similar-sized organizations that have recently done campaigns and you'll quickly determine what program is right for you.

Chapter VIII

If You Don't Know Where You're Going, Any Road Will Get You There. The Importance of Planning

You Want a Roadmap

You know you're going someplace, but not sure how to get there. You've signed a resolution, you know you're going to make a gift, and you hope that somehow everything will come together. But how?

That's why you've hired a consultant and/or a campaign manager. It's their job to create, with your participation, a clear and detailed plan to give you the confidence that you know where you're going and what you're doing.

Once campaign central is assembled, one of their first and most important asks is to create a campaign plan. This plan may be shown in a number of ways:

- A narrative, that describes the steps and provides the order in which they'll occur
- A detailed calendar, telling what will happen when and who will be responsible for doing it
- A timeline breaking the campaign down into categories and showing how the pieces fit together

Ideally, you'll be able to understand and follow the plan whatever your learning style. No one way works for everyone, but all board members and volunteers need to understand the theory and practice of the campaign.

What the Plan Lays Out

From the start, you need to know:

• Where money will come from (individuals, foundations, corporations, government, and others)

• What sizes of gifts you'll need

• The order in which you'll pursue different sizes and sources of gifts

• What collateral materials you'll need and when, and how PR will figure into the campaign

• What the construction schedule will mesh with fundraising

• What benchmarks you're going to meet

• How you'll continue to make your donors feel good about their gifts (your stewardship plan)

Every plan is different, but most contain the above elements, simply in different ways.

Sources of Funds

Every campaign should know from the start where the money is coming from. You need goals for board giving, other individuals, foundations, corporation, government, and other possible sources. While all campaigns will require the board to give, the proportion will vary, as discussed elsewhere. Proportions from sources vary wildly:

• Many organizations accept no governmental funds, relying entirely on private sources to complete their campaigns.

• Churches may rely totally on individual gifts; independent schools rely heavily on such support.

• Social service agencies can attract significant government support, but often have limited access to individuals and corporations.

• Art museums and metropolitan hospitals often have wealthy boards that provide a large portion of campaign proceeds; smaller arts organizations and healthcare facilities may have community-based, un-moneyed boards with limited giving capacity.

- In some organizations, staff campaigns are extremely important. Donors want to see what their doctors have contributed to the hospital campaign.

Whatever combination you hit upon, you must set goals by sector and have a clear idea of who your prospects are.

What Size Gifts Do You Need?

Long division is the biggest enemy of successful campaigns. You need $2 million to renovate your synagogue and there are 400 families in the congregation. "All we need is $5,000 per family" is such a logical way to approach the campaign.

But it will invariably fail. Why? *Because fundraising is not democratic.* People can't, don't, and won't give the same amount.

For some people $5,000 is too much. A young family trying to save to buy their first house, paying for daycare while the mother works at an entry level position, doesn't have $1500 a year extra to pay off a three-year pledge. Neither does an elderly woman, scraping by on social security. A per capita approach would lose members and make people feel bad.

But human nature plays a role as well. The young banker making $70,000 a year could afford a $5,000 gift over several years. However, when he thinks of one of the truly wealthy people in the congregation, he's inclined to think, "If this guy owns 13 fast food restaurants and a $5 million house and he's giving $5,000, why should I give the same amount?

What works for almost any campaign is proportionality. The person with the most capacity and connection gives the largest gift. People with less wealth and less connection give smaller gifts. There are always variations, but the shape of a campaign gravitates toward a pyramid:

- A few big gifts on top (remember the Rule of 12—the largest gifts that will make up at least 50% of the campaign)
- More gifts in the middle ranges
- Many gifts at the lower ranges

The Gift Chart

At the start of the campaign, you should have a gift chart that shows how many gifts at each level you need to reach your goal. This chart will provide you with simple, easy-to-track and understood goals. At any point in the campaign you'll be able to compare the gifts you've raised to those you've projected. This offers an easy way to judge your progress and chances for success.

Suppose that your $4 million campaign's success depends on receiving a single gift at $500,000, three gifts at $250,000, and eight gifts of at least $100,000, allowing you to fulfill the rule of 12—but just barely. However, after six months, you have no gifts at the two top levels, and several of the prospects at that level have pledged $150,000. At that point, you can see that your goal is in question.

On the other hand, if you've received a $600,000 gift, a $250,000 gift, and three gifts at $150,000, you can feel fairly well assured that your goal remains feasible. Your first five gifts total $1,300,000. Even if you receive only one more $250,000 gift, your top 12 gifts will still equal or exceed 50% of the campaign.

The shape of the pyramid varies to be sure. Sometimes the top gift is ten per cent of the goal, sometimes it's 25%. The top gift for a $5 million campaign might be $500,000 or it might be $1.5 million. The other largest gifts will vary according to the size of the top gift and the size of the campaign.

If your $5 million campaign relies on three top gifts of $500,000, you'll need several additional gifts of $250,000 to reach your goal. On the other hand, if your top gift is $1,000,000, you might only require single gifts at $500,000 and $250,000 to reach your goal.

Sometimes, extraordinary giving at a lower level can make up for fewer gifts at higher levels.

- A YWCA used the category of "Wonder Woman" to recognize all gifts of $10,000 or more. An unusually high proportion of campaign funds came from the 400 women whose gifts fell into that range

- An assisted living facility campaign attracted more than 100 gifts at $25,000 in response to a specific named giving opportunity. This lowered the requirements for gifts at the $50,000 level.

Sometimes campaigns decide that they don't have the need or opportunity to pursue many gifts at lower levels. They decide that such gifts are too expensive to raise, since they result from special events, direct mail, and other inefficient means of raising money. If organizations don't need to expand the number of donors, it might make sense to focus on bringing in a few more gifts at the higher levels.

In all cases, you have to create a plan that corresponds to the reality of your potential donors. If your wealthiest supporter can give $1 million, it makes no sense to create a plan dependent on a $2 million gift.

Equally as important, you have to always keep the "rule of 12" in mind. Your top 12 potential gifts have to make up at least half your campaign. If you're trying to raise $1 million, 12 gifts have to add up to $500,000 or more. If you're raising $50 million, your largest 12 gifts have to add up to $25 million. You don't have a gift of $7.5 million? Your chances of success are probably not very good.

The Constituency Chart

When you plan your campaign, you should know what groups of donors you will approach. In almost all campaigns, certain constituencies appear:

- The board
- Staff members
- Corporations
- Foundations
- Large gifts from individuals
- Smaller gifts from individuals
- Funds from public sources, such as federal, state, or local governmental entities

Your plan should indicate how much you expect to raise from each of these. Often, however, you will want to break down these categories (or constituencies) even further.

If you are part of a hospital campaign, your medical staff will represent an important constituency. If you are raising money for a local historical society, community businesses will be a separate constituency that represents community support. If you are raising money to expand an existing independent school, grandparents will make up one important constituency, parents of current students another, and alumnae/i another.

As the campaign progresses, constituencies offer another measure of your success. If you've planned to receive 20% of your goal from regional and local foundations, but discover that their gifts are likely to total less than 10%, you must reapportion your goals. Can you increase your corporate or individual goal? Are there ways that your board can increase its giving in response to lower foundation support?

Arranging your goals by constituency permits you to be very imaginative and encourages breaking up the campaign into smaller sub-goals with spread-out responsibility. Sometimes campaigns will create 12 or more constituencies, each with a separate and very achievable goal. This allows the campaign to see consistent, widespread progress. It also means that at the end of the campaign, you have greatly expanded both your volunteer and donor bases.

Then the Plan Has to Indicate Who You Go to First.

Most campaigns go to the board first, then to the biggest individual donors, then to foundations and corporations. But there are exceptions to most rules—other than going to the board first.

- A large art museum got very generous board gifts, which served as its lead gifts. While it received some corporate and foundation gifts soon after, it decided that it could maximize its campaign by demonstrating widespread support with thousands of community gifts. It adopted a "pig in the python" campaign model, with a huge bulge of donors in the middle and fewer, larger gifts at the head and the tail.

- An assisted living facility campaign went to a large number of major donors (in this case $50,000–$100,000) before it asked for its lead gift ($1.5 million). The potential lead donor did not want to go out on a limb before knowing that others in the community were also strongly behind the project.

When You'll Need Materials

As discussed at length in Chapter XI, you'll need fundraising materials and you have to expect to pay for those materials. You don't necessarily need them at the very start of the campaign. And, for your initial gifts, you may not need anything fancier than a two-page letter on your organization's stationery.

Your fundraising plan should lay out what materials you will need and the point at which you'll need them. Working back from the due date, you can then construct a schedule indicating when your decisions have to be made and when you will have to reserve time at the printer.

Sometimes you'll need materials for your board campaign, sometimes you don't. We recommend that you assemble a "Board Decision Booklet" that puts into a single place all the information you need to make a decision about your gift. But you may only need to see the campaign plan and a gift pyramid.

Your lead donors may or may not need completed materials before they make their gift. However, before talking with any donor, including your board, you need materials that demonstrate the following:

- The benefit to the broader community (however you define it) from your project
- An easy-to-understand budget that shows the projected sources and uses of revenue
- A description of what will happen in the building (known as a functional program) or as a result of the endowment, to enable a donor to understand what the building or endowment will do
- A clear and convincing explanation of how the organization will sustain its expanded operations
- A gift chart, so that donors can understand how their gifts fit into the entire campaign

Branding the Campaign

A campaign 'brand' (logo and/or tagline) can take hours or months to create. It's worth the effort to create something that is effective and inspires volunteers and donors.

- An agency that was building several facilities that would serve children had a very ambitious goal. They spent hours looking for the few words to encapsulate what they were trying to do. Finally, the organization's head of development blurted out, "Our city has given a fortune to the arts. They've built new sports stadiums. It's time to step up for kids." And "Step up for kids" became the campaign theme.

- An independent girls' school was proud of its graduates' success and the programs that created confident, self-assured young women. The public relations committee struggled for months to find a theme, until a parent said, "You're opening their horizons, so they can look forward to boundless success." It quickly became the "Boundless Success" campaign, featuring a silhouette of a confident girl carrying her books and laptop toward a successful future.

Your plan tells you whether you need a logo now, later, or never. It indicates when you have to reach out to your closest supporters, your second closest circle, and to the entire community. It defines your audience and outlines methodologies of reaching them.

Integrating Public Relations into Your Campaign

Later in this book, we will look at public relations in greater depth. In thinking about a campaign plan, it is vital to determine where you need efforts to increase public awareness. More important, however, is determining who your audience is.

Your potential donors may fall within a small circle. It doesn't matter if the entire community knows about your independent school campaign, as long as your parent body and alumni know.

If your donor universe is larger, however, publicizing the campaign can help create an atmosphere in which raising money becomes easier.

- A regional YMCA was launching a major campaign. They discovered that the community had an incomplete perception of who the YMCA serves and what services it provides. In response, they disseminated their annual report in the local business journal, reaching corporate decision makers. They also held a series of community forums that spread the word to the general public. The outcome was a heightened awareness and appreciation of what the YMCA does.

- Often public awareness offers little help with the general public, but swells the chests of organizational volunteers and makes them feel confident enough to ask others for support.

Your campaign plan should delineate the purpose of public relations, its timing, and the audience to which it is aimed. That audience can be as broad as the entire nation and as narrow as your membership. You should develop strategies to reach all major donor constituencies, not forgetting your internal supporters—your board, staff, volunteers, and others who may not be big donors, but will influence others. Your messages must be consistent with each other, but tailored to your constituency.

Your Construction Plans

Campaigns may precede construction by three months or by five years. A campaign for a birthing center started exactly nine months from the day it was due to open. A campaign for a museum started six years before construction started..

In every case, the campaign used the concrete timeline of the building project to motivate volunteers to get the fundraising to a pre-determined point.

In general, the single most important benchmark is groundbreaking.

- We recommend that organizations have at least 80% of the funds they need pledged before they break ground. If your total project cost is $5 million, your supporters should have pledged and/or given at least $4 million before you stick a shovel in the ground.

Once ground is broken, fundraising urgency abates for many people, since they assume you wouldn't have started the project without having the money to finish it. Volunteers begin to focus on the physical project rather than completing the fundraising for it.

Having 80% committed is pretty safe, since you will have other gifts in process and a few people will prefer to wait until they know the project is a "winner." But 80% is a minimum. Less than that and you risk running out of momentum before the campaign is complete.

Your contractor or project manager will create a project plan for construction. Your campaign manager and/or consultant should suggest other benchmarks for you to use in your campaign. These may be totally internal, such as moving forward to design documents (a very expensive step), or external, such as groundbreaking, topping off, or the grand opening. In all cases, they will help gauge whether your fundraising is ahead or behind schedule.

A Stewardship Plan

One of the most important truths to remember while you're in the midst of the campaign is that your fundraising is only starting. The money raised to create a building or an endowment is only a down payment on your future needs. If you look at capital campaign gifts as the ultimate gift your donors will ever make, your future is likely to be bleak.

Your goal is to ensure that every campaign donor becomes an annual donor, a prospect for future capital campaigns, and will want to cement their relationship by making a planned gift—leaving you a bequest or other gift from their estate.

Your plans for the future begin with the capital campaign plan. You should determine how to connect your donors to your mission and to demonstrate to them on an ongoing basis that their gift is allowing you to do a better job of carrying out your mission. Your success will gratify them and make them feel great about their gift and anxious to do more.

Your plan should outline communications and event plans that serve to tie your donors to you. They should share in your good and bad news and be asked to participate in all events marking your progress.

Equally as important, your stewardship plan should project past the opening, to ensure that donors remain involved:

- A donor to an open science lab at a museum was invited to drop by the museum to see the lab in use. He was delighted to see youths totally immersed in scientific investigation in 'his' room.

- A youth service agency communicated to a donor the results of the position her gift had endowed. The donor immediately (without any request) gave an additional gift to permit the program to be expanded.

The lack of such a stewardship plan can have devastating consequences:

- A regional theatre attracted more than 500 "adopt a seat" donors at $1500 each. For the two years after the campaign was over, the theatre didn't contact the donors, thinking that they should "give them a rest." Almost all of these donors stopped making annual gifts and many were never recovered. "They got our money and forgot about us," one of the donors complained.

Your plan may have more parts or fewer. In all cases, the plan shows you where you're going and how all the pieces fit together. You should be able to scan it at any time and determine how you're doing—whether you're ahead of or behind schedule.

Over the course of the campaign, the plan will change focus, adopt new strategies and tactics, and perhaps move goals between sectors. But these changes should be gradual and transparent. The board and steering committee should review and respond to proposed major changes, especially in the overall schedule and the size of the goal.

Your plan should be a living document that guides your actions and ensures that everyone knows where they are on your schedule. It should tell the story of how you're going to reach success. And the final campaign plan should be a history of where you've been.

Chapter IX

Creating the Materials You'll Need to Succeed without Wasting Money

Setting the Mood

Every car manufacturer creates beautifully illustrated glossy brochures filled with photos of their cars from every angle, often decorated with attractive models and placed in dramatic settings. They also have DVDs and other audiovisual aids to help you imagine how wonderful you'll feel in their cars. You can go onto the World Wide Web and see photos of the car and even get a price quote with the precise options you want.

Yet, few people buy a car based solely on these materials, without visiting a dealership or otherwise experiencing the auto firsthand.

Auto makers are pretty good at selling cars. Why do they spend millions of dollars on these tools when people are going to make up their minds based on face-to-face meetings?

They create the materials, of course, to establish the correct preconditions and atmosphere for a sale. By sampling their cars through the printed and video word, you get a feel for whether it's the right car for you. Part of it is the look and feel of the brochure—a Kia brochure looks and feels a lot different than one for a BMW or a Lexus.

Part of it is style. Cars for young people are more likely to have hip-hop music on the DVD than cars aimed at older folks. Trendy colors dominate ads for Gen Xers, as opposed to the primary colors aimed at older people.

And part of it is perceived expense. A brochure for a Geo is not going to be effective if it appears to be incredibly expensive, with embossed covers and die cut inserts. A Mercedes probably won't show up effectively in a skimpy brochure with cheap paper.

Your Project Is No Different

You need materials. Your potential donors need to be able to look at something that summarizes what you hope to do and how you plan to do it. They need to know your budget, both for the project and for its operations once it's open.

For appearances in front of the Rotary or Kiwanis, you probably need a brief video or slide show, especially for those who have difficulty in translating words into images without visual aids.

You need an identity, so that anyone receiving information about your project knows it's from you. You want to make certain that your newsletter doesn't get mistaken for a direct mail appeal.

But you don't need a Cadillac brochure to sell a Saturn. As a matter of fact, expensive, glossy materials will probably turn off potential donors to a grassroots social service agency. A homeless shelter won't have a high-power DVD with symphonic music swelling in the background and James Earl Jones providing the narration.

Your materials have to be appropriate to the project.

*What Do You **Really** Need to Establish the Merits of Your Project?*

To start with, you need a clear case.

This goes back to your feasibility study. During that process your potential donors and leadership reviewed your case and suggested ways to strengthen and improve it.

Now's the time to take their advice and create the most compelling, clearest, simplest case possible. Start by reducing what you want to do to its most important outcomes. "We're going to reduce homelessness by 25%." Or, "We're going to provide a venue for world class performers."

Then translate those outcomes into benefits for the community. "Our city will be a safer place to live." "Our kids will grow up appreciating the arts and be more likely to go on to college."

These outcomes and benefits will form the core of your case statement, because they will drive everything else you write. From them, you can derive the project description. You'll be able to relate what you're doing to true community needs and explain why your solution is best. You'll show how much the project will cost and how you will sustain it.

You'll feature stories that bring the project alive and that lend themselves to illustrations through photos, video, or drawings. Choose representative images. Don't fall into the trap of the large social service agency that had a diverse client base but created a brochure featuring dozens of cute little blond kids!

Once the case is finished, you can start deciding how you will showcase your project—which mediums will work best.

If many of your meetings are going to be one-on-one briefings, you might put your case and supporting materials into a "view book," an easily altered notebook that provides talking points. The view book is useful for those people who don't need to be impressed—just informed. Depending on how elaborate the view book is, it can cost $10 to $50 for each copy. Since it's only meant for a limited number of donors, it allows you to approach your initial donors at small cost.

You'll probably need a major donor brochure to share with a larger number of donors (for example, with all prospects for gifts of $25,000 or more). Such a brochure has about an 18-month shelf life and will be expensive to produce. It tells your story in an attractive way. More importantly, it gives you consistent talking points when you meet with donors. The brochure acts as a prompter, ensuring that you stick to the script.

Even more important, a well-done brochure lets you speak to prospects knowing that you've defined your project and that you have something that makes it concrete. In a sense, the brochure isn't selling **the prospect** on your campaign; it's selling **you** on your ability to present your case effectively!

The major donor brochure should be appropriate to the project.

- A humane society had their brochure design donated by a top advertising agency. It told the story of a dog at the shelter waiting to be adopted. It used black and white photos and effective typographic treatment and folded out to a long vertical strip. It was relatively inexpensive to produce and was printed on uncoated paper. Although the design was incredibly sophisticated and effective, the brochure didn't look expensive and donors loved it.

- A social service agency that provided treatment to juvenile sex offenders created a large format six panel brochure that was almost all photos and captions. It was on heavy, but rough, stock and used black and white photos and color highlights. It didn't look expensive and gave a sense of dignity and worth to kids who are among society's most feared and disliked.

- A science museum produced an expensive, heavily illustrated, die-cut combination brochure and presentation folder. It contained exhaustive information and room for additional materials tailored to the prospect's interests. While the look was appropriate, the content didn't describe a museum that was supposed to be fun and entertaining. Volunteers quickly stopped using it and thousands of copies finished the campaign in a closet.

To Video or Not to Video?

You probably want a video to give to people, to show at Rotary, or to stick in your laptop at the drop a hat when you meet somebody who's interested in your project.

Videos can now go onto cds and DVDs, are cheap to reproduce, and carry all the excitement of your project. Unfortunately, most people never stick them into their DVD player or computer. They don't hold up well for large audiences, and are either too long or too dull.

And they're expensive. A top-level video company will charge at least $10,000 for a four minute video, and as much as $50,000 for something longer and more elaborate. If you try to do it yourself, it will probably scream amateur.

Ask yourself whether you really need a video. What can a video do that you couldn't do better by talking about the project animatedly, supported by your brochure and perhaps comments from the executive director or program personnel?

A video works best if it tells a compelling story and focuses on an individual talking about how your organization affects them personally. You also need clear plans as to how you will use the video and how you can update it as needed.

Several organizations have put their video on their Web sites, allowing the public to view it on demand. They have reported good success with this approach, allowing prospects to get a fuller flavor of the organization even before a face-to-face meeting.

Other Collateral Materials

You will need letterhead, envelopes, a template for a campaign newsletter, note cards and matching envelopes, a pledge form, return envelopes, and other materials with the campaign logo and slogan on them. Your volunteers will want to recognize immediately what mail is from the campaign and what is normal agency business. Separate letterhead will give the campaign a sense of identity and begin the process of branding the campaign in the community.

Campaign materials frequently will morph into the agency's materials in its new home. Usually, the campaign materials are brighter, sharper, more tailored than the previous look, and fit with your new facility.

How Much Should You Spend on Materials for the Campaign?

Materials are as much a legitimate cost of the campaign as staff, consultants, and new telephone lines. You should ordinarily budget a reasonable amount for these materials, hoping to get at least some of the design, photography, and printing donated.

For almost any campaign of $1 million or more, you should plan to spend a minimum of $25,000 for materials. For larger campaigns, the costs increase. Social service agencies are less expensive than arts organizations. Health care campaigns are often expensive, in part because of the need to hire technical writers, and creating effective designs and diagrams to explain complex technologies.

In all cases, the cost for campaign materials fits within the overall campaign budget. Use the template in the appendix to determine how much your materials will cost (See **Appendix B**: *Sample Campaign Materials Worksheet*).

Final Thoughts on Campaign Materials

It is most important to get the campaign under way quickly and to maintain momentum once it's started. Nothing brings a campaign to a grinding halt quicker than arguments over campaign materials.

How do you avoid this?

- Determine that the top priority is to give your volunteers what they need to make their initial calls. They will soon realize that the materials are part of the supporting cast, not the star.

- Appoint a small editorial board, to which you entrust all decisions about campaign materials. Accept that you're not going to love everything they do, but trust them to get close enough to perfection to satisfy your needs.

The worst materials are the ones that get picked to death until they lose all life. The best materials are the ones that get you out the door and in front of potential donors.

Web Strategies

Most potential donors expect nonprofit organizations to have attractive, informative, easy to navigate websites. They click to your site to learn about you and often gain their initial opinion of your worthiness from a quick perusal of your site.

You should feature your campaign on your site. Since by definition your campaign is one of your top priorities, that significance must be reflected in your public portrayal of yourself. Your website can be an invaluable resource to your campaign. At the very least, it offers a way to describe what you're doing in words and images. You can include access to your brochure, video, architectural plans, and other materials.

You can also offer links to most media coverage and provide updates through a web-based newsletter. Equally as important, you can use the Web to collect names and contact information, expanding your prospect base. It's easy to recognize volunteers and donors on your Web site, as well as keep your constituents informed of your progress.

Solicitation on Your Site

Generally, it's counter-productive to use your website for soliciting campaign donors until the very last portion of the campaign. Your focus has to be on face-to-face requests of lead and major gifts until you enter the community phase of the campaign. Providing potential major donors with the opportunity to give small gifts without personal contact is almost always a mistake. Even if you use your website to solicit and receive annual funding, you should not offer the option of making capital gifts through electronic means until the last stages of the campaign.

Email Strategies

Most organizations are accustomed to communicating with their supporters by email. There are many campaign-related strategies that allow you to continue and expand this approach.

Frequent updates on the campaign can be sent to those closest to the organization. These updates should be brief, punchy, and make the recipients feel like insiders. Notification about large gifts, significant campaign milestones, and other 'breaking news' are all likely topics for such communications.

Chapter X

Who's Going to Give and Why—And Why You Have to Concentrate on Individuals You Know

An Embarrassment of Riches

During your feasibility study, you will have talked to several dozen (or more) potential donors and gotten a pretty good idea of where your top gifts are coming from. You'll also have received recommendations of who else should give.

You also have a long list of people who are already associated with your organizations. Depending on the type of organization, they may be members, subscribers, donors, volunteers, or affiliated in other ways.

For other organizations, you'll have lists of alumni, attendees, event participants, and other connections. Organizations have mailing lists that range from 500 to hundreds of thousands.

In every case, the same question arises: Who are our best prospects?

It's probably not Denzel Washington, Madonna, Bill Gates, Warren Buffett, the Rockefeller Foundation, Wal-Mart, or Tiger Woods.

Over the years, I've discovered that the favorite source to which people look for gifts is OPM—Other People's Money!

They assume that Willie Sutton was right when asked why he robbed banks. "Because that's where the money is."

And so they look to famous rich people, whether in their community or halfway around the world, to fund their project. They make that intuitive jump—that because a rich and famous person cares about kids and your project helps kids, the rich and famous will jump at the opportunity to fund your project.

Except, in all probability they won't.

We've all heard about the check from an angel that arrives unexpectedly, the free cars that Oprah gave away, or the huge gifts that Bill Cosby made to his alma mater. And we ask ourselves, "Why shouldn't we get those same gifts?"

Because there are millions of good causes and only a limited number of world famous people.

Take Bill Gates. He and his wife have a foundation with more than $30 billion in assets, which will grow as funds from Warren Buffett are absorbed. If they totally liquidated foundation assets and divided the money among America's 1+ million nonprofits, each would receive about $25,000. But the foundation has guidelines, with clear and well-considered priorities. He's unlikely to give to an Iowa museum or a small social service agency in Maine.

Equally as important, even with organizations that fit within its guidelines, a foundation wants to see initial gifts from those closest to the organization. They expect that the board, local residents, local institutions, and others who know the organization will make the first gifts and provide the majority of the money. For some types of organizations, the assumption is that those with close connections will give all the money. Most churches, independent schools, and organizations focused on extremely specialized interests fall within this category.

Outside funds will come in only if the organization has a proven community benefit, regional importance, and a strong track record of local funding.

Otherwise, your donors are people you know and who know you, who see the benefits of what you do either directly or indirectly, and who want to see you move to your next stage.

The truth is, you're probably starting off with too many prospects rather than too few, and your primary task will be to whittle down your list to those on whom you should focus.

What Are the Attributes of Your Potential Donors?

Three attributes define likely major donors:

- They care about you. They have some fundamental connection between their values and your mission.
- You have some influence over them, in terms of people connected to your organization whom they admire and will respond to.
- They must have enough money to make a significant gift.

How Do You Go about Deciding Who Your Best Prospects Are?

Start with the obvious.

You've done a study and talked to those people closest to you. In the course of the study, some people have stated that they would at least consider a significant gift. While the precise nature of these conversations is confidential, you will know enough from the study to identify who you should talk to first.

In terms of actual giving, your board gives first and they are the ones you can ask for true "stretch" gifts that use as much of their resources as possible to help you reach your goal. Their giving sets the bar for everyone else. They have a strong connection to your organization and would not serve on your board if their values didn't align with yours.

Next, you ordinarily go to your most generous current donors, those who give you major gifts now (anyone who provides at least 1% of your contributed income). You should have people within the organization who can reach out to them.

Next you think about those people who give every year and have given a substantial amount of money in total. Perhaps you should include anyone who has given a specific amount aggregately—for example, all those who have made gifts totaling $10,000 over the past five years.

Longevity of giving is also a good measure in determining who your best prospects might be. Anyone who has given during ten years out of the past fifteen might be considered a good prospect, whether for an outright gift or a planned gift (primarily a bequest).

Former board members, people who have at some point given you a large gift, and very wealthy people who have been modest donors are also obvious prospects.

But sometimes using these categories doesn't result in a usable donor list.

Sometimes you list all of these people and you either have too many prospects or too few. If you're a large social service agency, you might have 30,000 donors, of whom 5,000 fall into one of the categories listed above. Or you might be a small museum where only a few dozen people fall into these categories.

What do you do in these cases?

Too Many Donors

No matter how big your staff is, you can't know every one of your donors in a large organization. Even if you've met them, you might not know very much about them.

Two avenues are open to learn more about who gives to your organization:

- You can hire a service to screen your donors. They take all the names you give them and match them against publicly available data bases (stock holdings, home values, ownership of large boats or airplanes, charitable donations). After the screening, they provide you a listing meeting your criteria. Such screening is not very expensive and often provides valuable information. While capacity to give is no guarantee of an actual gift, it gives you confidence that there is money available. You can then priorities in terms of who your top prospects should be.

- For smaller numbers of donors, you can do research on what resources and interests they might have. By using publicly available data, you can find out a great deal about your contributors' worth, their interests, where they went to school, and to whom they donate. This helps you determine who might be your top prospect.

Too Few Donors

If you're trying to raise $20 million and you discover that you only have 300 donors, 600 members, 500 auction attendees, 14 board members, and a dozen donors of $1000 or more, your donor list is too short to give you much confidence in success. Since there's lots of overlap between these categories, you discover that your total potential donor list is perhaps 500 individuals. Going through the exercises listed above, you might only find a few dozen major donor prospects.

Your feasibility study indicated that your support was very narrow and very deep. A few people would give a lot of money, but there was no broad support to help you once you had raised the initial 60% of the campaign.

You have to become more creative at this point:

- Include lapsed donors and begin to decide which of them can be brought back into the fold
- Determine which donors might create family gifts, rather than just giving from their own resources
- Try to create challenge gifts or matching gifts, so that donations from foundations, corporations, or wealthy individuals stimulate giving by people now not part of your donor base
- Who are the people not currently donating to you who are passionate about your cause? For example, many wealthy people never use libraries, but they recognize the immense value they play in our society and are willing to support them.
- Who has given to similar causes?
- Are there businesses your project will benefit by attracting foot traffic?
- Are there local, regional, or national businesses that might create partnerships with you to attract additional funds?

And Then There's the Evaluation Task Force

No matter the size of your organization, you have a list of people you think might make sizable gifts. Depending on the organization and the campaign, 'sizable' changes. For a 200-family church congregation making a $1 million addition to their church, any gift of more than $10,000 is big. For an art museum raising $100 million, it might be $250,000 that defines "big." In between, the threshold might be $25,000 or $100,000.

In general, the more prospects you can find for your top gifts, the better. You can establish rankings of which gift you pursue first, but setting goals is important.

There is generally no better way to evaluate the ability and likelihood of a donor making a major gift than to assemble a peer group.

Who Should Be on the "Evaluation Task Force"?

Bankers, accountants, real estate agents, leading socialites, and your organization's development professionals all know a lot about your donors. Assurance of absolute confidentiality and a late afternoon meeting with good wine help with making people feel comfortable in sharing their knowledge.

They can review hundreds of names quickly. At the end, you'll have a list of qualified donors, listed according to the amount they can give and the likelihood that they'll make a gift. Your organization can then begin to decide who goes to whom.

This process is necessary even if you use screening, since it verifies that you have real connections to the prospects. Also, screening will not tell you if the prospect is in the midst of a nasty divorce, dying of cancer, is being sued by their partner, or just made a huge gift to another organization. Your task force can (and usually will) tell you all of those things.

What Do You Do with the Prospect List Once You Have It?

As the chapter on planning indicated, you need to assign each of the prospects to the appropriate committee. Then you rank them by priority, starting with the biggest gifts. If you have several gifts at the same size, a close friend with a long history who can give $100,000 is a better prospect than a person who could give $200,000 but has never been closely allied with you. The community will want to see support from those closely allied with your organization.

Otherwise, big gifts generally influence small gifts and take priority over them. Big gifts from highly respected community members are the most powerful of all.

The important rule is don't pursue a small gift from a rich person to start the campaign. It will set a low and harmful giving level. *Never forget that each gift is a campaign in itself and must be placed within the structure of the entire campaign.*

Chapter XI

It's Not Called a Steering Committee for Nothing

Roles of the Staff, Board, and Steering Committee

Leadership is key to any successful campaign. Ordinarily, this leadership comes from a steering committee composed of fierce partisans of your organizations who also are widely respected among the community you're relying on to support the campaign.

Leadership must also come from your staff and board during the campaign, even if they're not the most visible portion of the effort.

Staff Roles

Clearly, the executive director (president, administrator) is at the center of all you do. He or she must represent the organization, embody excellent stewardship of all funds received, and effectively interact with both donors and volunteers. In many campaigns, the chief executive spends half of his or her time on the campaign and is involved with all of the largest gifts.

The development department plays a vital role in the campaign, as discussed elsewhere, but it is a mistake to assume that they're the only staff members who are intimately involved with a successful effort. The entire staff is ordinarily asked to donate funds, participate in cultivation and solicitation efforts, and act, as appropriate, as spokespeople for the campaign.

Board Roles

Many organizations believe that their boards are "too weak" to lead capital campaigns effectively. Their boards cede the leadership role to the steering committee and expect a free pass in relation to the maelstrom swirling around them. Other than making a gift, they avoid the campaign and simply hope that others will make it work.

This is often a recipe for failure. The board, as the body with financial and legal responsibility for the organization, must also take on a strong supervisory role in a campaign. Along with making all policy decisions relating to the campaign, the board has to continue to serve as organizational safekeepers.

At least ten major responsibilities fall to each board member, whether or not they are members of the steering committee or actively involved in soliciting gifts:

1. Ethical stewardship—making certain the your organization lives up to its mission statement and behaves in an ethical fashion at all times

2. Resource management through investment in appropriate and high quality planning

3. Resource management through ensuring that campaign expenses are maintained at the proper level

4. Campaign management ensuring that the campaign does not begin until the proper preconditions are in place, including leadership and staffing

5. Quality control through ensuring that all campaign materials reflect well on the organization

6. Personal investment through making a gift that is significant to the board member—ordinarily one of the largest they have ever made, to reflect their passion for the project

7. Connections to potential donors and leaders, using your position and commitment to expand your organization's circle of influence

8. Advocacy for the project throughout the community

9. Involvement in any of the various campaign activities

10. Fiscal management of the project, to make certain that donors get the best return for their investment

Campaigns Succeed Because of Leaders

Leadership is the key indicator for success. If an organization can attract strong campaign leadership, they can make up for any other deficiencies. If they can't, the campaign will struggle.

The first step in establishing leadership is to recruit a powerful, highly committed chair or co-chairs.

Who Is (Are) the Chair(s)?

When asked what their greatest challenge is, most organizations cite the difficulties in finding good board members and other high level policy- and fundraising-volunteers.

This difficulty multiplies exponentially when it comes to recruiting capital campaign chairs.

What are you asking someone to do as chair?

- Make a big gift (it doesn't have to be the biggest in the campaign, but it has to be really big for them)
- Attend at least two meetings a month to maintain campaign momentum and unity
- Help recruit other steering committee members
- Help on major solicitations
- Attend a limited number of special events and provide inspiration to the entire organization
- Speak at local civic events, be available for newspaper interviews, and generally represent the organization
- Remind other steering committee members about their responsibilities and assignments

If it sounds like the responsibilities for a CEO of a corporation, that's no accident. Your organization is raising more money than ever before. You're involving more people than at any time in your history. The project is probably the most complex activity you've ever undertaken. Someone in the private sector would get paid a lot to run it. Your campaign chair(s) receive nothing other than personal satisfaction and recognition.

So, it's no wonder the person in charge has to be energetic, multi-talented, have excellent intrapersonal skills, and have the respect of everyone associated with the organization.

Do Such People Exist?

Every community has people that others respect and admire. They're not always the richest or best known, but

- They are seen as leaders
- They hold the best interest of the community at the center of all they do
- Others look to them for advice and counsel
- They are considered wise and fair

Those are the people you want as your chairs.

These people can be community volunteers, business leaders, respected professionals from law, medicine, accounting or other fields, or they may be from other fields.

Oprah probably won't chair your campaign; neither will Ken Griffey, Jr.

Professional athletes, well-known politicians, television or movie stars, or other celebrities tend to be too busy and have too many other pulls on their time to take on volunteer responsibilities. There are exceptions, but few. And "honorary chairs," offering their names but not their hearts, don't provide effective leadership.

In looking at campaign chairs, the most common traits are passion for the organization and its mission, the time to devote to the cause, and an ability to motivate other people. Possession of unquestioned integrity and a stellar reputation are characteristics shared by great leaders.

- A campaign for an assisted living facility was chaired by a commercial real estate broker whose mother had lived in the related nursing facility.

While not wealthy, he was known for his charitable activities. He was passionate about the organization and tireless in his pursuit of gifts. The campaign vastly exceeded its goals, in large part because of the chair's passion.

- A campaign for a science museum found a 40-ish executive as its chair. He had been successful in business, but had never risen to the ranks of a top community leader. Over a four-year period, he worked incessantly to complete the largest fundraising campaign in the state's history. At the end of the campaign, he emerged as a universally respected leader.

Campaign chairs have to possess great courage and a willingness to speak on behalf of the project. They have to be patient with the foibles of others, but possessed of a sense of urgency that inspires others to get their tasks completed.

Models of Leadership

Thirty years ago, the president of the local bank chaired the big campaign and called up his friends. This was the heyday of the "old boys' network." Those days are gone forever. Today, the chair or chairs of a campaign come from many different backgrounds, men and women, and represent several constituencies. Campaign leadership may not be as high profile as it once was and is certainly spread out more evenly among men and women, among the very wealthy and the passionately committed, and among people of different races and ethnic backgrounds.

Co-chairs may split the work. One chair may be very good at running meetings (an invaluable skill), while the other is good at public speaking. One chair may be well-connected in the business community, while the others are more involved with the town's social elite. Sometimes one chair is a political office holder or even a judge, who cannot actually raise money. They bring such prestige and integrity that their presence as chair attracts other volunteers who are willing to raise funds.

Sometimes, an unexpected chair is effective:

- In one campaign, a young female business executive took on the chairmanship of a campaign for a male-oriented organization. Her presence opened the doors to many women-owned businesses and to female philanthropists.

No one model provides certain success; a variety of structures can work. The key is to ensure that you have the ability to reach sources of large gifts, and that the chair engenders respect that will attach to the project.

"Contract" Chairs and Other Volunteers

Sometimes, you know that a potential chair or other lead volunteer cannot spend very much time on your campaign. They are too busy, out of town much of the time, have pressing personal issues, or are so frail that they don't have the energy to perform many of the normal tasks of a lead volunteer.

On the other hand, they would bring you prestige, connections, and other positive attributes. What do you do?

"Honorary chairs," exist primarily as an excuse for volunteers not to do anything. Most potential donors see through such "letterhead names" and disregard their involvement in a campaign. They know that it's easy to get someone's name without getting any of their soul.

Instead, it is more effective to use leadership contracts. In these documents, you list the precise tasks you hope someone will undertake on your behalf.

For example, a small social service agency wished to involve a former Congressman in its campaign. He was busy campaigning for elective office and was seldom available. They suggested that he could provide invaluable help by serving as campaign co-chair with the following expectations:

- Attend three major events and give "rah-rah" speeches (he was a great speaker)
- Help obtain two gifts from businesses to which he was closely attached
- Make a limited number of calls to public funding sources asking for support
- Give the featured speech at the grand opening

These tasks required a time commitment of perhaps 25 hours over a two year period. He agreed, performed beyond expectations, and was an integral force in the campaign's success. From his standpoint, the exposure he received was extremely positive and helped his political aspirations.

Such contract leadership arrangements result in almost universal success. Organizations receive high-profile leadership, volunteers get the satisfaction of helping good causes, and the community sees well-known people setting a good example.

The Steering Committee

During the feasibility study, you will have discovered people who think of themselves as possible campaign leaders and who the community perceives as ideal leaders. You will have identified possible campaign chairs and the potential members of your campaign leadership group—the campaign cabinet, senate, or steering committee.

The steering committee has many functions. Reporting to the board, they are the volunteer group that:

- Develops and implements campaign policies and strategies (the board has to approve any policies that relate to the organization's by-laws).

- Provides a public face for the campaign and for the organization during the duration of the campaign.

- Includes several of your lead donors who set the example for the entire community.

- Connects the campaign to other lead and major donors outside the board.

Overall, without a strong steering committee, your campaign will not succeed. If the people you're counting on for big gifts can't see a group of recognized leaders with credible track records, you will probably struggle to gain support.

The Rest of the Volunteer Structure

A sample campaign structure is in this book's appendix (See **Appendix F:** *Sample Org Chart*).

Campaign organizational charts should reflect the expected sources of campaign contributions, and the specific needs of the campaign.

- Large campaigns have more committees than small ones.

- Each specialized constituency needs committees or a sub-committee to work within those constituencies

- A building committee ensures the building doesn't outstrip its funding and provides ongoing management of the project

- Most campaigns need committees that focus on businesses.

- At the start of a campaign, you will need several short-termed task forces, including:

  o An evaluation task force that determines who can give how much to the campaign.

  o A public relations committee that oversees the campaign's public awareness efforts, including its publications

  o A gift acceptance and recognition committee that oversees creation of policies concerning what gifts can be accepted and how they are acknowledged and recognized.

- For campaigns that rely in part on public funding, there may be a committee that focuses on this area. The committee will create strategies and coordinate their implementation, as well as help make contacts with governmental decision makers.

- For large campaigns, you will need separate committees for various levels of giving—one that focuses on the top 30–50 gifts, another that focuses on the middle range of gifts, and a third that focuses on the smallest level of gifts you will be soliciting face to face. You may also need committees or sub-committees for more narrow constituencies— a local business committee, or a physicians sub-committee.

- If you plan to approach the entire community for support, you will need committees or subcommittees that focus on special events, house parties, the sale of mementos, and other means of attracting support.

How to Recruit Volunteers

It is one thing to ask someone for money. All they have to do is decide yes or no and say how much.

It's another thing to ask someone to make a commitment to help a campaign reach its goal. You're asking someone to spend time, risk their reputation, and put their entire being on the line. That's commitment.

Just as you wouldn't ask someone for $100,000 over the phone, you're not going to request someone's ultimate commitment in a note or email. You're going to prepare to meet with them and have materials that explain what is expected. You have to be totally open and honest about their roles and responsibilities.

For important positions early in the campaign, the board chair and executive director should make the call; once you have a campaign chair(s) in place, they should be involved in recruitment. Ideally, one of the reasons you've recruited the chair is for their ability to attract other top leaders.

What do you need when you visit with potential leadership candidates?

- A detailed job description that lays out responsibilities and expectations, including time commitment and financial expectations and a brief, easy to understand project description, so that they know what they're supposed to represent

- A list of others involved in the project, including your board and any volunteers you've already recruited

- A budget both for the organization's operating budget and the capital project. You must show that you have costs in hand and have a stable financial base

- For "outsiders," your organization's annual report and/or audit

- Any campaign literature you've already developed

- A campaign organizational chart, so they can see where they fit in

Just as in requesting funds, there are no magic words. You have to go into the meeting with optimism and be willing to answer any and all questions. You have to listen carefully and be prepared to alter your plan.

If your potential leader shares your enthusiasm for the project and expresses a willingness to take on the challenge, they will make a successful volunteer. If they say that they'll do it, but only because they're being a good sport, you won't really be able to count on them. It's better to seek out your second choice than to accept a half-hearted commitment.

Leadership makes or breaks your campaign. Passion is the secret ingredient. The best campaign volunteer wakes up every morning thinking about what the campaign needs for success.

Chapter XII

Recognizing Gifts

Sometimes Thanking People Isn't Enough

Every gift is a good gift.

No—make that a great gift. It is the largest gift that the donor can make at this moment. It is a testament to their generosity and a lasting connection to your organization and its aspirations.

You can never thank someone enough for their gift.

At the minimum, as soon as a gift is made official by signing a pledge form, the "thank yous" should start. The board chair should jot a quick thank you. The executive director should write a thank you. Whoever solicited the donor should send a thank you. The development department or campaign office should send a thank you, along with the official acknowledgement of the gift's value. While oral thanks are never out of place, written gratitude is much weightier.

The gift should be entered into your gift processing system. If it's a pledge, there should be a tickler system that reminds you when to send a reminder that the payment is due.

But for many board members (and others who are going to give to the campaign) this is the biggest gift they have made and the biggest gift they will ever make. It may represent the equivalent of three months salary, or the value of a new car, the cost of a dream vacation, or even the cost of a second home on the coast.

Many people want and deserve special recognition for their gifts.

They want to have something to point to when they take their children or grandchildren to the building when it opens. They want a permanent connection to the building or endowment, so that in fifty years people receiving the benefits of the structure or the fund will associate their gift with this project.

A gift to a capital campaign is one path to immortality (or at least a big chunk of time when your name will be up in front of the community).

How many people would remember Carnegie without his libraries? Getty or Guggenheim without the Museums? Stanford without the University?

Those sorts of recognitions exist at tens of thousands of other sites throughout America and the world. If you visit Ephesus in Turkey, part of the ancient Greek empire, you'll find the names of patrons on the temples. If you look at many of the great religious paintings of the 15th century, you'll see small portraits of patrons included in masterworks.

Think of your town and the names of people that are on buildings, in art galleries, on walls in your church, or at the entrances to your parks. In all likelihood, you respect them as community leaders, and are aware of their contributions to your personal enjoyment. You may think that you'd like to someday have your name on a building or in a room at the local library, so that your descendants can look with pride at the contribution their family made to your town.

Or you may have no such desires for recognition, but want to honor a parent or a favorite teacher. Haven't you ever thought how wonderful it would be to dedicate something to someone who helped you reach your current position in life?

Not everyone wants or needs recognition, but it is sufficiently universal that it serves both as an impetus and a reward for giving. Donors stretch a bit to reach a level high enough to earn permanent recognition. They see their gift as meaning more if it's attached to naming rights, whether for themselves or others. The community sees the entire project as enriched and enhanced by its association with their leading citizens.

Establish Your Policies Early

While many board members don't need any additional incentives, some will want to know what type of named giving opportunities are available. Take the time at the start of the campaign to establish your policies.

What are you trying to accomplish through named gifts?

What's the lowest level for permanent recognition?

What's the lowest level for any type of public recognition?

How do you value gifts other than cash or pledges? Are their any rules about planned gifts? Will you recognize bequests that may be withdrawn?

Your development department and consultant will help you craft policies that keep you out of trouble. A gift acceptance policy will mean that when someone wants to give you a Ferrari Testarossa that isn't street legal, you have a reason to either refuse it or assign it a value that reflects the difficulty you'll have in selling it. It will mean that you can turn down time shares in Zimbabwe or vacant lots in swamps. You can have rules about acceptance of polluted properties.

The policies should cover all fundraising, not just raising money for the capital campaign. They should be appropriate to your organizational culture, giving your board some flexibility in special circumstances and acknowledging that it can't foresee every eventuality. But the main thing is to have your policies in place before you ask anyone for money. It'll save a lot of problems.

So How Do You Determine Named Giving Opportunities?

Let's assume you are building a new high school as part of a k-12 private school. The building will house 300 young scholars, most of whom will go on to college. The parents of these children are extremely status conscious and drive their kids to school in expensive cars and live in large houses, primarily in gated communities.

The total cost of the high school is $12 million, of which $9 million is for the actual construction and the remainder consists of soft costs—architects fees, permitting fees, state and local sales tax, fundraising costs, and other expenses.

The school will include 15 classrooms, three science laboratories, a media resource center (what used to be called a library), a 300 seat auditorium, a small chapel, a faculty lounge, student lounge, and two music practice rooms.

You have, of course, created a gift chart—that mysterious grid that guesses at how many gifts at what size it will take to complete your campaign (See **Appendix D**: *Sample Gift Chart*). You know that you'll need at least one gift of $1.5 million, two gifts of $1 million, four gifts of $500,000, and eight gifts of $250,000.

So, that means that to name the building, someone has to put up $1.5 million, which becomes your top naming opportunity.

Wrong.

If you set up your named giving opportunities that way, it means that no one has the incentive to give more than $1.5 million. The family that just sold its business for $100 million will not have any reason to provide you with a $2 million gift. Not only that, but for whatever reason, most people are shy about taking the top level of gift, fearing that they're either being made a dupe, or that they'll appear to be showing off.

The Italian Leather Sofa Theory of Named Gifts

Go into a furniture store where most of the sofas cost $2,000 and you'll generally notice that there's a really expensive sofa, sometimes soft Italian leather, totally impractical, very beautiful, on sale for $5,000. You sit in it, luxuriate in the soft and supple leather, and appreciate the lustrous finish. And then you feel really good about spending $2,000 on a much more practical, almost as handsome sofa that fits better with your house, your golden retriever, and your pocketbook. Although you had wanted to spend no more than $1500, seeing and rejecting the $5000 Italian leather sofa makes you feel very secure in getting a good deal.

Named giving works the same way. Maybe no one will ever take the top naming opportunity, which in this case might offer naming the entire campus for $3 million. They might not jump at the chance to have the Appelbaum campus at the Country Day School.

They might, however, find naming the High School to be a bargain at $1.5 million. Naming the auditorium for $1 million would be an absolute steal, since generations of kids would go down to "Appelbaum" for their assemblies.

On the other hand, someone will see the $3 million and think it's not worth it to get the campus name, which they don't think will really stick. But for $2.5 million, they could name the High School for their parents and the auditorium for their in-laws, so they'd have the Teitelbaum Auditorium in the Appelbaum High School at old Country Day.

The same principles work at lower giving levels for smaller projects. Enlarging a hospice by eight rooms and adding a sitting room might cost $1 million. The top gift might be $150,000, with other gifts needed at ranges of $10,000–$100,000.

If you set the Italian leather sofa gift at $250,000 for the "reflection garden," no one might take it, but they might see naming the facility for $150,000 as a wonderful way of commemorating a favorite grandparent.

Setting the 'Coin of the Realm.'

In most campaigns, the most common major gifts will not be at the very highest level. If you want to raise $6 million, you'll probably need several dozen gifts at $25,000 and even more at $10,000. You'll want to encourage people who have never given more than $1000 to aspire to a new level.

Named gifts or gift clubs often provide the necessary encouragement. People who have never given major gifts before come to the realization that there's a difference with a bigger gift, in terms of how you pay it off and what you receive in return. The naming opportunity is one more way of reminding a donor that this is a different kind of gift—one that involves leaving a legacy.

- A nursing home decided to add an assisted living facility. The gift chart showed the need for at least 50 gifts at $25,000 or more. The facility included 110 apartments for residents. The campaign decided to offer small, tasteful naming plaques for each room, recognizing gifts of $25,000. By the time the campaign ended, almost all of the rooms had names attached to them and the additional money allowed an upgraded facility.

- The New York Public Library had famous people host a series of small dinners. Admission to these parties, at the apartments or homes of opera stars, well-known philanthropists and/or art collectors, and other celebrities, cost $50,000. It also meant that you gained permanent recognition on the Library's donor wall and set yourself apart as a donor of significance. The perceived prestige of attending one of these dinners helped convince many people to make gifts larger than they might have otherwise.

What these examples hold in common is success in establishing a high level of giving as a norm. To be recognized as a significant contributor to these campaigns, you had to join a large number of people making gifts at a specific level. The number of people who have given at that level made it seem natural to be considering a gift more than you'd ever made before. It created a club you were joining and allowed you to feel part of an important group

When Named Giving Is Inappropriate

Sometimes, named gift opportunities don't work. You can't name a church, although you can name a chapel. At some private schools, status seeking is a major gaffe and no one wants their name up on a wall. Some ethnicities or religions prohibit any type of personal recognition or ostentation.

Then what do you do?

- A small private school that abhorred any type of personal recognition simply put up a dedicatory plaque that read "Thanks to all our supporters."
- A research center allowed donors to have favorite literary or Biblical quotations inscribed on pavers
- A historic church attached small plaques to pew bottoms
- A confidential shelter for battered women had a statue with the single words "Thanks" inscribed at the base.

You always obey the donors' wishes, but at the same time seek ways to acknowledge their generosity. If they don't want personal recognition, you find other ways to indicate how thankful you are for their gift. If they don't want any recognition or acknowledgement, you accept their wishes.

Donor Walls, Bricks, and Other Ways to Recognize Smaller Gifts

At the start of most campaigns, someone will suggest some form of a brick or paver campaign. "We have 100,000 people in town. I'm sure we can get 5000 to pay $100 for a brick—and that's half our campaign right there," they'll say.

Neither the assumption nor the arithmetic works.

Without massive publicity, tremendous advertising costs, and personal salesmanship, you can never get 5% of a town or city to do anything. Campaigns that have succeeded in selling thousands of bricks generally have had media sponsors, coupons running in newspapers for months, and other donated (or paid) publicity. Not very many campaigns either merit or afford such an investment.

Equally as important, this approach forgets how much the actual bricks and inscriptions cost. Often, the cost of creating such an entry level naming opportunity approaches 50% of the donation, a poor use of donated funds.

There are reasons to do such broad-based forms of recognition:

- Your project truly touches almost everyone. The tile campaign at Seattle's Pike Place Market attracted 35,000 donors. It made a clear statement that the Market belonged to the entire community
- You want to make sure that everyone has the chance to be part of the campaign
- You have a huge current donor/subscriber/member base that you can reach easily and repeatedly to offer them the chance to buy a brick
- You have almost no donor/member/subscriber base and need a means to establish a base of support once your building is up

Be aware that such a campaign is not an efficient way to raise money, so that your motivation for doing a brick or tile campaign has to involve more than a financial goal. There are better ways of attracting large numbers of donors that will be addressed in a later section of this book.

Intermission:

How Money Gets Raised

Chapter XIII

Some Things Your Mother Never Told You about Asking for Money

You May Never Have to Ask (At Least the Way You Imagine It)

Your mental image of asking for money might entail sitting down with your good friend Martha and, after a glass of wine or two, asking her for $50,000 toward the new community pool you're working on. You feel nervous tingles in your stomach, you start worrying about what Martha is going to ask you for (she's on the board of your church), and wonder whether you'll ever be as good friends again if she makes the gift. Worse yet, will you remain friends if she turns you down?

The truth is, if you do your job correctly, you'll never have to worry about any of these things and you'll probably never actually make the request the way you imagine. You simply have to redefine your job.

Your job is not to ask for money.

It's to deepen the relationship between people you know and the project to which you have committed yourself. You are a matchmaker, a conduit for support to a great project.

According to the *Chronicle of Philanthropy*, almost all Americans (more than 90%) regard themselves as charitable, making an effort to support those less fortunate at some time of the year. They give to projects and organizations they believe in and make large gifts to those that touch them deeply.

The main challenge they have is distinguishing amongst all the competing charitable organizations. They get dozens or even hundreds of appeals annually. How can they tell which organizations are truly worthy of their support?

By hearing from people they trust.

That's where you come in. You are involved in your project because you believe in it. You've shown that belief in three separate ways, at least:

- You are serving as a volunteer and providing your time.

- You have made one of the largest financial gifts you've ever made.

- You're willing to involve other people by asking them to serve and give.

Most importantly, you are approaching them as a peer and a friend, saying that in your best judgment this is a project they might care about. You have nothing personal to gain from their gift, since your only interest is in the completion of a project that will provide benefit to the community.

There is no reason for you to feel any sense of guilt or to believe that you're "using" your friends by inviting them to become involved and committed in the project. You are doing so only because of your own commitment. There is no direct advantage to you in having them involved. You are acting out of altruism— a belief in doing good for the entire community.

But why won't you actually have to ask for a gift if you do things correctly?

Because your goal is to connect people to the cause, not to ask them for money. Their gift will follow naturally from that relationship, rather than from your request.

If you follow the procedures suggested here, you'll get to the point where your friend will say, "I want to help. What can I do?" At that point, they're prepared to give and simply need guidance. And as a trusted friend, you can suggest what would be an appropriate level of support they might consider.

They will agree or suggest another figure. They will establish the terms of their gift, in terms of payment period and method of payment. They will be doing it because it makes them feel good and because they have sufficient information to know what their gift will accomplish. Making the gift will help them achieve their most deeply-held values. If your project does not correspond to their beliefs and values, you'll never get to the point of talking about a gift. At some point they will have said, "This isn't the project for me. I'm glad you gave me the chance to learn about it, but I have other priorities."

You will know that they respect and like you, perhaps even more than before. They will be making their decision based on their needs and desires, not yours. This is why basing all fundraising on the donor's needs is so central—it places the focus on them, not you.

Establishing Meaningful Relationships—The Importance of Cultivation

Cultivation works on gardens. You plant seeds, carefully keep the soil watered, weeds cleared, the plants staked if necessary. Your care and labor are rewarded by healthy plants and eventually by fruit or flowers. If you just toss the seeds in the ground and return after months of neglect, you're more likely to find a weed-filled, scraggly spot with neither fruit nor flowers.

But dating may be a better analogy. You generally don't propose on a first date, no matter how wonderful that first date. You have to spend time learning about the other person; recognize their interests, strengths, and frailties; permit them to learn about you; and then, after months or years pop the question. By the time you ask to marry them, you're assured of agreement.

That's closer to how cultivation works. You introduce someone to the project (or perhaps to the entire organization). Over time, you provide them with the opportunity to learn whatever they want to about what you're trying to accomplish. You learn about them at the same time—their values, concerns, and hopes. Over time, the relationship deepens and it becomes obvious that it's time to ask for a significant commitment.

What are the varieties of cultivation possible during this type of 'dating?'

- Special events are one obvious type of cultivation. If people come to your auction, benefit, or testimonial dinner, they will see who else supports you. They'll get some information about your mission and programs. It's easy to follow up after the event simply by calling them and inviting them for a tour of the organization they've already been part of.

- Tours of your facility offer a perfect opportunity to acquaint someone with your organization. No matter what your organization does, you can make it a "behind the scenes" tour, showing them things most people never see. Whether it's the costume shop at your theatre, the collection space at your museum, the chem lab at the college, the archive at your church, or the new surgical suite or cardiac lab at the hospital, you can show them something special.

- Lunch or other structured meetings that are set up to introduce them or deepen their knowledge of your organization and its project provides an excellent cultivation opportunity. You and the executive director can provide information and answer questions.

- Program participation lets people see exactly what you do. Service at the homeless shelter or food bank, chaperoning at a school dance or volunteering at the annual auction, or giving a guest lecture at your college all connect people to what you do.

- Sending people targeted information after they know a little about you often deepens their interest and answers their questions. A letter from the executive director bringing them up to date on recent progress, or a note from one of your clients telling them how they were helped by the organization helps people understand the nature of your activities.

- Inviting them on a travel opportunity creates time for them to learn more about you. International aid organizations often take prospects for site visits; museums take prospects to major shows in other cities.

- Inviting prospects to serve on a task force, whether it's to help plan your marketing efforts or to get advice about your building design, strengthens their bonds with you and your mission.

Cultivation possibilities are limited only by your imagination. Some, like those listed above, are intense and require planning and time. Others are simply touches:

- Sending birthday or anniversary cards
- Forwarding interesting news stories about your organization and its accomplishments
- Including them on an "insider newsletter"

- Sending them a copy of your newest publication
- Sending them complimentary tickets

Your Goal Is to Spur Interaction, Not to Inundate

When you have identified someone as a potential donor, your temptation is always to pour as much information into them as possible. You love what your environmental organization is doing to preserve wetlands and you want the prospect to know about every acre that's been saved.

But that's not how people make decisions. They want to know what's in it for them. People want to know how your project's success will make them feel good. Will it increase the property value of their lot? Will it gain them recognition? Will it bring more tourists to the region?

People are skeptics. They are always seeking reasons why projects can't or won't work. They bring preconceptions and doubts to the meeting with you. If you swamp them with information they can't get their questions answered.

Who can be involved in cultivation besides you?

The **CEO** of the organization is always a good participant, because his or her presence adds weight to the visit. The CEO also demonstrates that the project is in good hands; in addition, your executive is generally the primary keeper of the vision for your organization and can speak effectively about the project.

The **director of development** can often be a valuable member of the cultivation team. The position can provide technical advice about how to give, discuss the nuts and bolts of the campaign, and offer the big picture view of fundraising.

The **campaign chair and/or board chair** is always a good participant in cultivation efforts. They bring weight and seriousness and show respect for the donor. It's preferable if they know the prospect, but they are always appropriate, since they are the highest level of campaign participant.

If your initial volunteer participant has never previously given a gift as large as what you're seeking, **another major donor** can be helpful. It's easy for them to mention, "I never thought I'd make a $100,000 gift to anything, but the YMCA is so important to our community that it's the best investment I've ever made."

Some people will be impressed if **a business or community leader** meets with them. Bringing along the mayor, your state representative, or even a local celebrity makes the prospect feel important and lends credibility to the project. It's also a good way to cultivate the person you're bringing along.

It is often extremely effective to include a client, student, grateful patient, or other **beneficiary of your organization** to meet with donors. Witnessing on behalf of the organization is powerful, since they are speaking from direct experience.

The **men and women who provide your services** are often the ideal partner for the top volunteer and the CEO. A professor, physician, social worker, or other direct providers can establish a strong link to a donor and ensure that the discussion focuses on the organizational mission.

The **consultant** is seldom an effective member of the cultivation team, since they are a "hired gun" being paid for their services, and having a vested interest in the project's success. They are not working exclusively for your organization. While they should be involved in creating strategies for each prospect, they are seldom the right person to lead cultivation efforts. The only exception may be with large institutional donors who wish to know about broader campaign strategy issues and understand the role of consultants.

How Do You Get Started?

There is only one key action needed to move things forward.

The first phone call.

That first call ensures that everything follows easily and naturally. The call results in an initial meeting. The meeting generates follow up, additional meetings, more follow up, and eventually a discussion about a gift and a decision. The distance from the first phone call to the gift can be weeks or years. But there's only one initial phone call.

Preparation Is the Key

Before you make the phone call, you have to prepare.

Why are you calling this person? What major objections might they raise? How will you respond to their initial objections?

First, give yourself a pep talk:

> *This is a terrific project. I've made my gift, so I'm not asking for anything I haven't done myself. We've planned the project to death and there's nothing that _____ can ask that we can't answer. I'm part of a great team.*

Next, remind yourself why you're calling:

- You are asking to meet with your friend/acquaintance, business colleague.

- You are calling to let him/her know about your excitement/interest/ involvement in a great project.

- You are calling because you think this person will be interested in the project, want to hear about it, will have valuable input.

- You are part of a fundraising effort, but this first meeting is not a request for money.

Think what your friend might say and some suggested replies. The important thing is not to hear no when your friend is not saying no:

- *"I'm very busy"*

  "Yes, I know you're busy. When would be a good time for us to get together?"

- *"I've given a fortune to the Boy Scouts and don't have money for another gift"*

  "I'm glad you're supporting the Scouts—it's a great organization. This conversation isn't to ask you for a gift—although you might decide you want to make one once your pledge to the Scouts is paid off."

- *"Just send me the info"*

  "I'll give you the brochure when we meet, but I'd much rather tell you why I'm excited about this."

- *"You don't need to waste your time. I'll just send you $50."*

  "I hate to turn down a gift, but it's important that you understand the impact this project is going to have on the whole community."

- *"I've heard about that. It'll never get off the ground."*

  "You're not the first person I've had say that—and you'll be delighted to know how far we've come."

Then remind yourself that your goal in this phone call is not to convince them, not to correct their misconceptions, not to get a gift, not to get permission to mail them a flyer. *It's to meet with them face to face and talk with them about the project.* Your answer will reflect this desire.

You're not going to debate, argue, or deny. You'll just focus on the desire to get together and share with them your excitement.

The meeting should be at a time and place convenient to them, scheduled to last for no more than an hour. Are they close enough to the project site that they can meet you there? Is there a private club where you can meet? Do they have a conference room at their place of business where they'll be away from their phone? Do you want to meet with them at their house? Play a round of golf or go to a baseball game?

Make Sure Your Voice Sounds as if You're Glad to Make the Call

Before you call, have your spouse or someone from the fundraising committee listen to what you're planning to say—at least for the first few calls. Make sure your consultant provides some real, interactive preparation that includes role playing.

Get used to sounding happy about asking for that first meeting. If you sound as if you're ashamed to be making the call, your friend will be reluctant to meet with you. He or she should feel that the meeting is going to be fun—not heavy or difficult.

Assume Your Prospect Will Accept the Meeting

An overwhelming percentage of people agree to meet with you.

Why?

- Because they respect you and believe you when you say they'd be interested in something

- Because, believe it or not, not very many people are so passionate about a cause that they want to meet in person to tell a friend about it—your friend will be impressed by your enthusiasm

- Because they're flattered and honored that you'd take the time to meet with them in person

- Because most people are charitable and are interested in the best places to put their charitable contributions

Don't try to hide why you're meeting. Don't say you want to get together to show them pictures of your grandkids and then spring a cultivation call on them. If you're proud of what you're doing for the project, they'll be happy to meet with you.

Decide beforehand whether you want to meet just with them or with their spouse, business partner, or other co-decision-maker. It's important that the entire decision-making unit feels included in the process, since the chances for a large gift are compromised if you've ignored one of the principals.

If the meeting is more than a few days away, let them know you'll be emailing them to remind them about it. In other words, treat this the same way as you would an important business meeting. Your prospect will appreciate the respect that reflects.

Preparing for the Meeting

Preparation for calls is often fairly generic, since you're interested primarily in obtaining a meeting and want to avoid getting into a lengthy conversation about the project.

Getting ready for the meeting is another matter.

In the appendix, you'll find a meeting preparation form that reviews what you need to do before a meeting (See **Appendix E**: *Call Preparation*).

The preparation should be thorough but focused:

- If you're going with another person, define the role each will play. If one of you is closer to the prospect, that person is the primary partner and leads the discussion.

- Determine the minimum and maximum acceptable outcomes for the meeting. The minimum might be for the prospect to agree to take a tour or meet with one of your clients. The maximum outcome might be that the prospect expresses enthusiasm and asks for more information about a specific aspect.

- Define the three most important thoughts you want to convey during the meeting:

  o *Our project will double the number of kids we serve*

  o *We think it will cut crime downtown by 50%*

  o *It'll save our city $100,000 in a year in reduced vandalism and minor crime*

- Prepare yourself to answer your prospect's most likely questions. What are their concerns? Do they worry about loss of tax revenue if you're turning an abandoned grocery store into a theatre? Will they be concerned about your ability to sustain your operations in a bigger facility? A successful preparation concentrates on what your prospect might ask rather than on what you're going to say.

- Decide what written materials you want to take. The first meeting is too early to take a proposal, but you might want to take your major gifts brochure as a convenient way to discuss the project. Some prospects might respond to a presentation on a laptop, or they may prefer a formal flip chart presentation. Do what will be most effective for them.

- Spend some time considering what question you most hope they will ask and what question you hope they won't ask. Prepare responses to each.

- Don't prepare a script!!! Be spontaneous and natural.

What Happens at the Meeting?

No matter how much you tell yourself that it's just friendly meeting, there's no getting around the fact that a cultivation meeting is somewhat artificial. You and the prospect know why you're there and where this is all leading. Small talk seems strained. There's a desire just to get through with the process and get to the point.

Resist that urge. People take time to make decisions, they need more information than one meeting can provide, and they don't like to feel pressured.

Start by thanking them for meeting you. Then talk a little about family, the local baseball or football team, other common interests. Let your voice relax and remember that at the base of it all, you're friends or business acquaintances.

When you've exhausted small talk, make a definite switch to the subject at hand. Acknowledge why you wanted to meet:

> *You've been a subscriber to the theatre for years; we wanted to bring you up to date on our capital campaign*

> *I know how important education is to you. We're doing some exciting things at the community college and I'll glad to have the chance to bring you up to date.*

Ask them what they know about the project and what their initial reaction has been. If they give a global response such as "It seems terrific," then ask them what most appeals to them. If they say, "It'll never work," ask them why they think that.

These meetings are the time when you begin to educate people. When someone indicates opposition, your task is to address their concerns, not to make them feel stupid.

- A homeless shelter located in an old hotel decided to build a completely new facility in a different neighborhood. A potential donor initially dismissed the project as a waste of money, because it would be cheaper to rehab the current building and the clients would trash the new facility. The volunteer showed that the building was so decrepit that it could not be economically renovated. He also demonstrated that because of better construction, insulation, and other factors, the new facility would be cheaper to heat and cool. The executive director then cited research that indicated that clients were actually more respectful of attractive, new facilities, that such facilities increased self-esteem and recovery rates. The prospect eventually made a $100,000 gift based on his new-found belief that the shelter would be foolish not to relocate.

- A human services agency was planning to consolidate its 15 leased locations by constructing a new headquarters to house both administration and programs. A prospect said that they would never recover the cost of building it. The board chair was able to demonstrate that savings on rent would both finance a loan for much of the cost and permit program expansion. Operational savings, especially in terms of saved time, would also support added programs. The prospect made a lead gift and has remained a donor to what he refers to as "a really businesslike agency."

These responses go back to this book's initial chapters citing transparency and a focus on the donor as the bases for ethical fundraising. You must assume that if donors know everything about your project, they'll agree that it deserves support.

Your project has to be an open book to your donors. You're asking them to give one of the largest gifts of their lives. It's imperative that they have the information they need to make a well-founded decision that makes them feel comfortable.

Your discussion should give you an idea as to the strongest interests of the donor.

- A nursing home was expanding and renovating its building. A potential donor responded negatively initially, stating that "You're creating this beautiful facility, but nobody's going to be able to afford to live there." This statement led to a discussion about endowing the facility to ensure that less affluent people could use its well-regarded facilities. The prospect made a $1 million gift to the endowment.

- A university was constructing a center for the visual arts. A prospective donor brought up during the discussion that her son had been "a disaster" until he had taken courses in computer-aided design, which had led to a successful career. The new center included a specialized classroom for CAD and the prospect jumped at the opportunity to make a named gift in support of the project.

Frequently, despite your best preparations, a prospect will ask a question you can't answer. It may be a reasonable question, a maddening question, or an off-the-wall question. Your job is to respect the motives of the donor, rather than assume that the question is either stupid or denies the project's merits.

Never be defensive.

Never imply that the question doesn't deserve an answer.

The only proper response is, "You know, no one has asked that before. I'm as interested to find out the answer as you are, and I'll get in touch with you as soon as I get the answer." Be grateful that this has given you the perfect next step in your cultivation.

End the Meeting by Setting the Next Step

Don't leave a meeting without some form of closure. Before the meeting you'll have established minimum and maximum expectations—now's the time to determine where you are.

If there is more than one person making the call, know whose job it is to set the next step into motion. That person must decide whether you're ready to pursue your minimum or maximum expectation, or something in-between.

Now that you've heard about the changes we're planning to make at the Humane Society, we'd love to have our chief canine specialist show you around our facility to illustrate the difference the campaign will make.

It seems as if you need some additional information. Can we send you some material addressing your concerns and then call you to set up another meeting?

Why don't we plan to meet again in two weeks or so, after you've had the chance to talk the project over? We can answer any other questions you have [this is for projects like building a new church, when all congregants know they're going to be asked for a gift and are already familiar with most of the plans].

When It's Time to Ask

It might be after you've answered all their questions. It might be after they've attended your annual auction, had a tour, studied your materials, and met your director of operations and CFO to discuss sustainability. It might be after you've had over six or eight different rounds of golf during which they've moved from skepticism to excitement. It might be when they've discussed the project with their financial advisor.

They're ready to make a decision.

But they may not volunteer a gift or suggest a number. It's your job to make a formal request. Generally speaking, it's time to ask for a gift when:

- You feel that you know their motivation for giving
- They have stated enthusiastic support for the project and indicated an interest in being part of it
- They know everything to make a decision
- The conversation has shifted to a discussion of your organization's mission and vision rather than focusing on the physical project itself.

How to Ask

You've reached the moment when it's time to ask, or at least to discuss the gift. Perhaps your heart is beating a bit more quickly than normal. Your throat may be a little dry.

But you're prepared. You and your partner have decided who's going to ask—and if it's you, you've stood in front of a mirror and practiced the words.

You know three things:

1. How much you're going to request
2. Whether you will use any props in making the request (the named gift chart or a gift chart)
3. How you will phrase the request.

Making the Right Request—Specifically

Let's start with the first element—that you're going to ask for a specific amount. Before you even met with the prospect, you received an evaluation of what you hoped they would give. As your conversations with the prospect had progressed, you were able to gauge whether that initial target amount was the right level, too high, or too low. The prospect has provided hints as to what he/she is thinking, and your staff and consultants have done research to back up the amount for which you're asking.

It may seem awkward or presumptuous to ask for a specific amount. You might think it's easier to either "let the donor make up their own mind" or to negotiate an amount.

In fact, more than 100 years of experience in American fundraising (and several thousand before that) show that donors prefer guidance as to what the right size gift might be. People don't want to make too large or too small a gift. They want to know how their gift fits into the entire campaign. Once they have an idea of what is expected, they can decide how much they will give, but the initial guidance is helpful.

Experience has also shown that few people are insulted or put off by a request for more than they feel they can give, as long as the request is made respectfully and after careful preparation. They do not always meet your request amount, but most are secretly flattered that you considered them at such a high level.

You should never, however, make a request with the expectation that the donor will give half or one-third of what you request. Your request should reflect what you think the prospect could give assuming they are as excited and enthusiastic about the project as you think they are. Setting out a specific amount is actually more comfortable than not, because the donor is clear about the magnitude of gift you are requesting.

Using Props

You will know, before the meeting, whether the prospect is ready to make a gift. You should arrive at the meeting prepared to respond when they ask, "So, how much are you going to ask me for?" Or when they say, "Gladys and I have been talking it over and we really would like to support this initiative."

Even with such an opening, it's sometimes difficult to get the words out when you're asking for a $100,000 gift (or a $10,000 gift) for the first time. There are a number of ways to make it easier.

The first is to make certain that you have brought a **written, formal proposal** to your meeting. Your staff and/or consultant should have worked with you to tailor every major proposal. The person with whom you're meeting should feel that they are the only person who could possibly receive this specific proposal. Of course, the proposal will include an amount, which obligates you to say the same figure.

A second prop is the **list of named gifts**. If you're asking someone for $100,000 to establish a named endowment to support museum education, pointing to that item on a printed form will let the donor see where their gift fits in. They'll see the relative value their gift will have. And you don't have to actually say the number if it makes you too uncomfortable—as long as your finger isn't shaking when you point.

A third prop is the **gift chart**, illustrating the number of gifts at various sizes needed for you to complete the campaign. Especially if you're working within a self-contained organization like a church or independent school, it's easy to show the prospect that you have six gifts at $25,000 already, and their gift would make seven, against a goal of 10 gifts at that level. Again, this avoids saying the number and lets the donor see that others have made gifts at this level already.

A fourth prop can be your **honor roll of gifts**, on which all donors are listed by name. You can indicate that their friends x, y, and z have each already given at the $10,000 level, and that you're hoping they will give at that same level. If your name is among those who have given at that level or higher, it makes such a request even stronger.

How You Phrase Your Request

There are no perfect, magic words.

Ideally, they will have already let you know that they plan to give, and it becomes a discussion rather than a request. In any event, you should avoid any sense of entitlement ("We know you can do a $100,000 gift and we're looking forward to listing it on the honor roll"). You should avoid questions that can be answered yes or no ("You'll make a $10,000 gift, won't you?").

Find a way that reflects your relationship with the prospect and shows that you're leaving the decision up to them:

> *My $50,000 gift to this campaign is the largest I've ever made. I truly hope you'll consider a gift at that same level.*

> *You've been a valued supporter of the hospital for years and you've often said how grateful you are to have such a fine hospital in the community. Your gift of $250,000 would help ensure that we can have the best and most modern equipment in our emergency department.*

Relating the gift to a specific outcome is also effective, if you know that the prospect has a specific interest:

> *Your gift of $50,000 will permit us to widen the stage to accommodate bigger, better, and more professional casts in our plays.*

> *Your past support of the First Generation Scholarship Fund has allowed many deserving students to attend our college. An endowment gift of $120,000 would fund two full scholarships every year in perpetuity.*

You can also use the most simple and straightforward request imaginable:

> *We would be most honored if you and your husband would consider a gift of $35,000 for our campaign*

The response is almost always some form of hesitation. If it's not and the prospect says, "Absolutely, I'd love to do that," you know that you've done everything right, that you've asked for an amount the prospect expected. You can then effusively thank them and hand them the pledge form.

Most of the time, the prospect will say something like, "My God, that's a lot of money!"

Knowing When to Keep Quiet

You've just asked for a whole bunch of money. Certainly more than the average person earns in a month. Often more than most people earn in a year. And occasionally, as much or more than many people make in a lifetime.

You made the request in good faith. The prospect has made gifts of this size before. They have the assets available to make a gift at this amount, over a three- to five-year period. They are excited and interested in your project and believe in your mission.

They've heard the amount. It takes time to absorb a request for a large amount of money. Few people make a habit of giving five-, six- or seven-figure gifts.

The last thing they want is to have someone interrupting their thoughts with a bunch of apologies or fallback positions. They can make their own decisions. Your job is to keep silent unless the prospect says something that requires your response.

Let's say you've requested a $50,000 gift.

After an initial gulp, the prospect says, "I just made a big pledge to the library campaign. I can't do this now."

At that point you can say, "We're not asking for a gift right now, just a pledge. As long as you can start your payments within the next three years, a pledge is just as good as a gift."

Or perhaps they'll say, "I can't write a check for that much money."

Your answer is very simple—"We're not asking that you write a check. Our pledge period goes up to four years, so it would only be $12,500 each year."

Perhaps they'll say, "That's more than anyone is this community has ever given."

And you'll tell the truth, replying, "That's true, but then, this is the most important, largest campaign in our community's history and a lot of people have given the largest gifts of their lives—I know I did."

The common thread in all these statements and responses is that the prospect is not saying no. They're just making a statement that you are duty bound to agree with. Your task is to reframe the impediment.

The worst thing you can do is immediately jump to saying, "Well, it is a lot of money. Do you think you can do $10,000?" They haven't said no and they haven't said the gift is beyond their capacity. You have to respond to their concerns, rather than hearing a refusal when none is intended.

Sometimes People Want to Give Less than What You've Requested

You are asking people to consider a gift at a specific amount. Sometimes, for whatever reason, that amount is more than the donor wishes to give.

They will usually be clear about this:

I'm sorry, but that's more than I'm prepared to give at this time.

I wish I could do more, but it's not in the cards.

Your response to this should be to leave the decision up to them. Don't suggest a number, because you're not a mind reader. Instead, ask what amount they would like to donate.

I'm glad you're willing to consider a gift. What level would you be able to consider, given a four-year pledge period?

And sometimes (although it's very rare when you've been talking with someone for many months and at several meetings), prospects will decline to make any gift:

We've been praying over it for the past several months, but we just can't make a gift.

Your response to a flat refusal must be gracious and immediate.

Thank you so much for allowing me to acquaint you with the project. I've enjoyed our conversations and I hope you'll allow us to keep you informed about the progress the project makes. You're an important part of our success.

Never take a refusal personally. Accept it at face value. They have thought hard and can't make a gift or don't wish to make one; they're not rejecting you. Don't guess at their motives or question why they continued to discuss the project if they weren't going to make a gift. You never know what will make them change their mind in the future.

- A campaign co-chair played golf every week with a wealthy friend and requested a gift during one of their rounds. The friend refused the request, but they continued to play golf. The co-chair kept up his enthusiastic chatter as the campaign reached 50% of the goal, 70%, and finally was at 90%. Every few months, he'd repeat his request for a $1 million gift. Finally, the friend agreed. "I never thought you'd make it, but it looks like you're going to succeed. I got stuck once giving an early gift to a project that never got built, and I wanted to be sure this would really go."

Sometimes They Can't Give an Answer

It takes most people time to make a decision about such a large gift. They might have to ask a spouse or partner if he or she isn't present. Or discuss the gift with a business partner. Perhaps they need to talk to a financial advisor.

Your response to their desire to put off a decision should be matter of fact and straight forward, but truthful.

We're trying to qualify for a challenge grant and they're making a decision in three weeks. Do you think you might have a decision by then?

Can I provide you with any more information to help you make the decision—are there any unanswered questions?

When would a good time to get back to you be?

Make sure you get a decision date that they agree to and make clear that it will be your responsibility to call them. If possible, schedule another appointment, whether by phone or in person.

You should make sure, however, that you aren't pushing them to make a gift before they're ready. They should make a gift on their schedule, not yours. While you can mention an upcoming benchmark or challenge that's time-sensitive, that is really your concern, not a motivation for them to rush their decision.

The Pledge Form

Every campaign needs a pledge form that allows the donor to record the amount of gift, the terms of the gift (restrictions, payment schedule), and to sign it. Donors often also specify recognition expectations on the pledge form, including a desire to remain anonymous.

Pledge forms are considered legally binding and are accepted by banks as evidence of intent to give. Lending institutions require pledge forms be signed before they will make loans against a fixed percentage of total pledges (often 70%). Donors should sign a pledge form even if they are handing you a check for the full amount on the day they decide their gift. An example of a pledge form is included in the appendix, but you should design your own and have it reviewed by an attorney (See **Appendix G**: *Sample Pledge Form*).

It is imperative that you require all donors to sign pledge forms. It formalizes the gift and ensures there is agreement on details. The donor should get one copy, a second copy should be held in your files, and the form should be scanned into your server.

Pledge Forms at the Solicitation Meeting

A donor has not made a pledge until the form is signed and the blanks filled in. When the prospect agrees to a gift, hand them a pledge form to fill out and sign—or for you to fill it out per their instructions and then give to them to sign.

If they are not ready to make a pledge or gift, do not leave the pledge form with them:

- They will lose the form.
- They will fill it out for a much lower amount than you have requested.
- They will agree to a gift, sign the form, and mail it back to you.

The third outcome is the rarest.

It's easy to say, "I don't want you to worry about the form until we meet again. I'll bring it after you've decided on your gift." It's also respectful, since you're expressing a willingness to make a special trip to meet with them again.

When the Prospect Announces a Gift

Every gift is a good gift.

Every gift is a good gift!

Respond with joy to every gift, no matter what size. Never forget that for the donor, this is the largest gift they feel they want to give at this time for this project.

Never imply in any way that the gift is too small or give any indication that you're disappointed. Remember that fundraising is about the donor's needs and wants, not yours. If making this gift now makes them happy and gives them a sense of satisfaction, avoid anything that interferes with this feeling.

Remember that this gift is the start of a deeper, stronger relationship. A small gift now may turn into a huge gift down the line if you meet their expectations.

And, as stated above, no matter how many times you thank a donor, it's not too many

In addition to formal notes sent by those involved in a solicitation, board members should be informed about any extraordinary gifts, so that they can thank the donor either by email, a note, or the next time they see the donor. The head of one of the nation's largest foundations remarked, "I am so touched when board members take the time to thank me for a gift. You'd be surprised how often we never hear anything except a form letter, even for a million dollar gift."

Some Last Thoughts

The process described here works because you are matching your cause to your friends' values. You are not forcing them to give or manipulating them. You're telling them about a project you support and offering them the opportunity to find the same happiness and satisfaction you have.

Although giving is exquisitely personal, it results from following the processes outlined here. You will succeed if you engage in a disciplined and supportive set of activities. If you try to ask people without cultivation, try to rush them, or otherwise ignore the advice contained in this chapter, your results will both disappoint you and deprive your friends of a joyful opportunity.

Knowing what you now know, you're prepared to embark on the fundraising portion of your campaign. Good luck!!

Part Two:

The Campaign

Chapter XIV

Why the Board Gives First

After the Bubbles Are Gone

You've had the Champagne or beer, you've signed your resolution of support, and your friends have toasted you for your bravery. It's the week after. It's time for the board to give.

What Does Commitment Mean?

The central element of board commitment is accepting the fact that you have to take on the ultimate responsibility for the success of the campaign. This means:

- However talented your executive director is, the ultimate onus for the campaign rests on your shoulders. You can't be spectators.

- The board has to make the basic decisions about the campaign, including scope, staffing, construction, and financing.

- The board has to steward the funds spent and received, follow campaign progress, and demand success.

- The board has to offer the community unrelenting unity and a positive outlook.

- The board must advocate for the organization and its plans, both in public venues and in private conversations with your friends and colleagues.

Initially, However, Your Commitment Comes with Dollar Signs

The board gives first.

Its gifts set the tone for the entire campaign. Generous board gifts determine how much other community members give.

Board members are the people closest to the project and the ones who best understand its significance to the community. If they hold back in their support, others in the community will sense that board support for the project is tepid and their response will be equally tepid. Generous, enthusiastic board support will establish a high benchmark for giving.

The board's giving will also set the stage for the campaign in a second way. It is essential that board members give only after careful consideration and after being solicited face-to-face by their peers on the board itself. Establishing this methodology of requesting gifts personally, requesting specific amounts, and following effective fundraising approaches will create the base from which the remainder of the campaign will spring.

How Much Should the Board Give?

More than you think.

Many consultants quantify the expected board gift by trying to make hard and fast rules. "The board should give 10% of the total." "For arts campaigns, the board has to give at least 25% of the goal." And so on.

These rules are great, but they bear no relevance to reality. The best answer I've ever found to "How much should the board give" is *An amount that will impress the community and convince them that the board is 100% behind the project.* A foundation executive who oversaw giving away millions of dollars annually stated, "I look to see if the board has a gleam in their eye—then I know they've stretched!"

Every board member has to give an amount that is significant to them, ideally the largest charitable gift they have ever made to anything for any project. This shows commitment.

I have heard every excuse as to why individuals don't feel that this applies to them.

"I'm already giving my time."

"No one really will ever ask what the board has given."

Forget it. If you don't give, when you are closest to the project and have nurtured it from the time it was only an idea, why should anyone else give? How can board members call on the community for support if they haven't made gifts that community members perceive as generous and even ambitious?

The first rule, absolutely inviolable, is that every board member must make a gift. The alternative to not giving is leaving the board. Having a non-giving board member advertises to the community that the organization is not unanimous in its support of the project. Many foundations and corporations will not make a gift unless all board members have given.

The second rule is that the board's aggregate gift must be commensurate with the community's perception of the board's wealth. A wealthy arts board will give a larger aggregate gift than a social service agency's board filled with community volunteers. But each board can have a positive effect on community perceptions by exceeding expectations.

Some Examples of Effective Board Giving

- A technical college board thought they might give a total of $50,000. After lengthy discussions and soul-searching, the gift reached more than $125,000. This not only got the $1.25 million campaign off to a great start, but made board members realize others could give significant gifts as well.

- An ethnic museum undertaking an extremely ambitious campaign (almost $25 million) had a small, young board. To their own (and everyone else's) surprise, their aggregate gift reached $500,000, with enthusiastic, rapid 100% participation. The size of the aggregate gift stunned the foundations, three of whom stepped forward with gifts much larger than they had initially contemplated.

- On the less positive side, an arts organization board composed of community, social, and business leaders decided that they did not have to make lead gifts for their extremely large campaign to succeed. Although they achieved 100% participation, the total board gift was less than 2% of the campaign goal, with the largest gift $500,000. The community sensed the tepid enthusiasm level of the board and the campaign languished.

So This Still Doesn't Answer the Question of How Much <u>*Your*</u> *Board Should Give, Or How Much You Should Give*

The answer lies in process.

Start by forming a "board giving committee," charged with evaluating the board's ability to give and assigning an aggregate gift goal.

The committee should have about one-fourth of the board's membership on it, usually including the board chair and other highly respected board members. This group meets and, in a highly confidential ands respectful manner, evaluates the ability of their colleagues to give. They take into account salary, stock holdings (if known), any matches from the company at which they work, family wealth, and any other considerations. Past giving history, both to your organization and to others, is also important.

The gifts for which you ask will be provided in the form of a pledge, payable generally over a three to five year period. Most people will not give the largest possible gift unless they can spread it out over at least three years. Five year pledges allow board members to give even larger gifts.

Gifts to capital campaigns are from assets, not your checkbook. If you want a rule of thumb, most people can donate a total of 1% of their net worth to charity each year. If you assume they're going to provide a substantial portion of that amount to your campaign, you can feel comfortable in asking people for between one and three percent of their net worth in a pledge to be paid over several years. If someone is worth $500,000, that translates into a pledge of at least $10,000 and as much as $25,000. If their company matches, that could make it a $50,000 total gift. Things add up quickly if you're imaginative!

Once all members are evaluated, it's time to add up the total. It will invariably surprise you to see what the potential giving amount reaches through this method.

Of course, not everyone is going to give at a maximum level. But some people will make unexpected gifts. If the campaign lasts three years, you'll have new board members to add to the total.

So—take your total of potential gifts. Make certain that you leave room in your goal to accommodate your largest possible gift (if someone can give a $1 million gift, you don't want to set a $750,000 goal).

Once the committee reviews and evaluates each board member (other than themselves), it's time for *them* to make their gifts. The board chair and the executive director and/or the consultant evaluate the other committee members before the board chair asks them for their gifts.

But before that occurs, the board chair gets to make his or her gift. Who asks? Sometimes, the chair simply makes the gift without solicitation, but sometimes he or she wants some guidance. At times, the consultant participates in the request, or sometimes the campaign chair, if it's someone other than the board chair. Sometimes, it's a highly respected former board member.

This is also the time for the executive director to make a gift. He/she will be asking board members to make a gift and must play by the rules—you must give before you ask.

Executive directors can literally make or break a campaign by their gift (by executive director, I'm covering whoever is the highest ranking staff person. It might be the rabbi, the university president, the managing director of a theatre company, or the administrator of as hospital. The title doesn't matter. It's the person seen as being 'in charge').

- A hospital CEO earning half a million dollars annually (or more) has to give a significant gift. While $25,000 might be a generous amount, it will mean that staff physicians, board members, and other executives in the community will not see the person in charge setting the campaign as a priority for themselves. And they will find out how much he or she gave!

- A gift of $25,000 from the head of a small social service agency who earns $60,000 annually will motivate his or her board and others associated with the organization. It will announce that the campaign truly matters.

Once the committee members make their gifts and receive some fundraising training from the consultant or campaign manager, it's time to meet with each board member.

Why a Meeting?

For two reasons:

1. Meetings make certain that you answer all of the questions a board member might have and make it more likely that the board member will give generously.

2. Your campaign will depend on asking for every significant gift during a face-to-face meeting. Every board member should experience such a meeting so they know exactly how it feels to have to look someone in the eyes and either ask for a gift or respond to a request.

Who's at the Meeting?

Ideally, two representatives from the organization (two board members or a board member and the executive director) meet with the board member and possibly his/her spouse or partner. This combination guarantees that all questions can be answered and all decision-makers are represented. The meeting should be in a quiet, confidential place. It might be in your fellow board member's house, or office, an office at the organization, or a quiet corner of a restaurant where the tables aren't too close together. You should be able to talk in a normal, conversational tone, with as few distractions as possible, with about 45 minutes for the discussion.

This is the time to discuss all of these issues and make certain that your colleague can enthusiastically support the project to the community, in addition to making a gift. It's also the time to make certain that he or she has all the facts and is communicating accurately with others in the community.

Once you answer all the questions and run out of nice things to say about the director, it's probably time to ask for a gift.

One of the easiest ways to ask for a gift is to cite your own example:

Natalie and I thought about it for a long time, but we finally decided we could do $25,000 over the next four years. I hope you and Felicia would consider doing the same.

Another way to ask for a gift is to mention the total goal and place their gift within that context:

> *We're hoping the board can come together to make a $1 million gift. To do that, we figure that four of us are going to have to show leadership with gifts at $100,000 each. Three of us have done that and we're asking that you consider being the fourth.*

Asking fellow board members for a gift is easy, because they're already sold on the project, probably know most of the details, and know that they're going to make a gift. You may find much of the advice in the preceding chapter useful for your colleagues on the board as well. You should feel confident that your meetings with other board members will be successful and productive.

After the Board Has Given

Ideally, you should be able to wrap up the board campaign within six weeks of when you start. Whatever you've reached, you should celebrate and thank everyone for their gifts.

If you've not made your goal, still celebrate and start making plans as to how you're going to eventually reach it. Think about including former board members in the goal, or future board members. Start thinking quietly about whether any board members might have slight misgivings, that will disappear as the campaign moves forward and they can make a second gift. Think about whether any of them might have a ship coming in over the coming months or years. Are they part of an IPO? Are they in the middle of the sale of a house?

Don't lower the goal yet. That's a last resort.

Instead, be proud of what you've got. In all probability, it's the most the board has ever given and will provide the base for moving forward.

What Happens If the Board Campaign Flops Totally?

If you get pledges for less than 50% of the goal you've set for the board campaign, something's wrong. Your board lacks belief in the project or has severe remorse about embarking on the campaign.

Now is the time to address these issues. It's one thing to set a board goal of $1.5 million and get only $1.3 million in pledges. That's a pretty good amount to raise and says that the board cares. As the campaign moves forward, new board members join, and current board members become more invested, you'll reach and surpass your board goal.

But if the board members have given a total of $500,000 from a $1.5 million goal, you're in trouble. It's almost inconceivable that you were off that much in your evaluation. It shouldn't matter how skilled you were in your requests.

Your board is simply not sold on the project. Their gift doesn't match up with how you (and the outside community) see their capacity. They will be unable to look the collective community in the eye and ask for large gifts. The community will be too likely to ask, "If you don't care, why should we?"

We recommend putting the campaign on hold, despite the embarrassment (and money) this will cost. You need to delve into why the board campaign failed, perhaps using an outside facilitator (not the consultant).

A failed board campaign almost certainly guarantees a failed campaign, so you would be foolhardy to proceed without repairing whatever is wrong.

But most board campaigns succeed beyond expectations and get the campaign off to a great start. That's when the real fun starts, because you can go out to the community and begin seeing the esteem in which the organization is held—and how effectively you can leverage board support.

Chapter XV

A Lead Gift Refers to More than Just Timing

Let's go back to the feasibility study, assuming you did one.

It indicated that there were at least a few people who would be willing to consider making top gifts to your campaign.

For a $100 million campaign, that might be gifts of $1 million or more. For a $5 million campaign, it would be a gift of $100,000 or more.

Ideally, the study indicated that there was a person or two willing to consider a gift at the very top of your gift chart—that $15 million gift for the $100 million campaign, or the $500,000 gift for a $5 million campaign, or the $150,000 gift for a $1 million campaign.

Once you've decided to move forward with the campaign, it's time to get serious about making that potential big gift a reality.

Why the Lead Gifts Are So Important

In all likelihood, however big your campaign is, it's the largest fundraising effort your organization has ever attempted. You're nervous about reaching your goal, despite the feasibility study and your bravado in signing a resolution of support.

People in your community are wondering as well. Can you achieve that audacious goal you've set? It's one of the most ambitious projects in the history of your town, or one of the biggest arts projects, or the biggest social service project. There are always skeptics, ready to spread uncertainty and pessimism.

People take your optimism with a grain of salt. They've seen other projects fail. "I'll believe it when I see it" is their attitude toward your goal, whether they say those words or not. No matter what the size of your campaign, it's a steep mountain looming before you and involves hard work, good fortune, and all the other intangibles if you are to succeed.

There's only one thing that will still the chatter, and convince everyone that you can climb the mountain and reach your goal.

A lead gift or two or three.

The Rule of 12

By now you've noticed that this book isn't much on rules or certainties. It doesn't decree that your organization can only raise three times its annual budget during a campaign. Or that you need to identify four prospects for every gift you hope to get. Or any of the other ratios that are accepted wisdom in the field. The reason why those rules are absent is that they're usually wrong. Some organizations raise 20 times their annual budget, while others reach their goals getting gifts from 85% of their prospects.

But one rule is borne out by experience.

Your top 12 gifts will make up more than 50% of your goal. If you're raising $1 million or $100 million, at the end you'll find that a dozen gifts make up at least half of the campaign.

The Collins Group has done more than 170 campaigns and almost never seen the rule broken, except when it took fewer than 12 gifts to make up half the campaign. A $180 million campaign had a $25 million gift, another at $15 million, and eight more at $5–15 million, totaling $90 million. A $1.2 million campaign had a $250,000 gift, and another 11 between $50,000–$150,000, totaling $750,000.

In almost every case, the rule holds. If you can't get those top twelve gifts, the campaign is in mortal jeopardy.

The "It's gonna happen" Gift

Within your twelve top gifts, there's usually one that calms everyone down and let's them know the project is going to work.

- Seattle wanted to build a new Symphony Hall. The board adopted an $85 million goal and the community gasped, because it was so much larger than any previous arts campaign. The campaign seemed to be going nowhere and the whispers were getting louder when the Symphony announced a $17 million lead gift. Immediately, the whispers stopped and people starting talking about the Hall as a reality, not a dream. A gift representing 20% of the goal gave the community the signal that this campaign really mattered and was something special. It continued onto great success and provided Seattle's superb orchestra with the hall it coveted.

Many other campaigns receive a gift like the Symphony's—a gift so large compared to the size of the campaign that no one can any longer doubt the project's ultimate success.

- A local technical college received a $250,000 gift for a $1.2 million campaign, after struggling for months to get fundraising under way. The lead gift inspired volunteers, gave the community confidence in the project, and unleashed several other gifts of $50,000–$125,000.

Sometimes a lead gift comes from a board member, where it has even greater affect on the campaign. It tells the community how important the campaign is to the board, while also establishing a target for other major donors to aim at.

- A hospital in a city of slightly more than 100,000 set out to raise $5.5 million. A local philanthropist made a $500,000 gift that astonished the rest of the community and made the project seem realistic. The hospital eventually surpassed its goal and attracted two other gifts at the same level—none of which would have been possible without the initial lead gift.

Sometimes a lead gift can be used to define the entire campaign and to raise its significance for the community. An unexpectedly large gift can enable an organization to undertake a bigger campaign than what they had initially conceived.

- A small museum in a suburban area found in a feasibility study that it could raise $8–10 million, but that this amount would permit them to build only a small facility outside the town's central core. There was a sense that a larger museum in the town center would "put a 'there' there," and have a catalytic effect on regional growth and self esteem. To do this would take $20 million or more, plus the initial funds for purchasing a downtown site. A local couple made a $2 million gift, quickly matched by the city, making the bigger museum a reality.

What Does the Need for a Lead Gift Do to Campaign Strategy?

Let's assume that you are raising $5 million for a new church. You think that there are five families that might make gifts of $250,000, but only one that can give $1 million.

The potential $1 million donor is perceived as being far and away the richest family in the congregation and during the feasibility study indicated a responsibility to give the biggest gift. They've said to a number of people on your steering committee, "We know everyone's looking at us." The range they indicated during the feasibility study was the big block on the gift chart that contained possible gifts at $250,000, $500,000, and $1 million. They declined to be more specific, saying that "our gift will depend on a lot of factors."

So—this gift and the other four could make up 40% of your campaign. How do you maximize the amount they give, and make them feel good about their gifts? Who goes first?

The answer is that you talk to your lead donor first. He or she will set the level for everyone else. If they give $250,000, the other families will give less, because they will feel that since they have less capacity, they shouldn't be expected to give as much. If the lead donor gives $500,000, some of the others will perhaps give half that, others less.

Let's turn it around for a moment, and imagine going to one of the $250,000 potential donors first. Imagine how the conversations in the house of Donald and Dorothy will go in discussing their gift:

Donald: Well, Harry and Hermione haven't made a gift at all yet and without them in the game, we'll never get to $5 million.

Dorothy: Yes dear and no one would ever complain if we made a $50,000 gift. It's still a lot of money.

Donald: But we'll never build a new church if we don't give more than that.

Dorothy: If Harry and Hermione haven't given, why should we?

Donald: I guess you're right. But we can do $100,000 and that'll look better.

Dorothy: If you say so, dear.

Without the guidance of a lead gift, Donald and Dorothy will give a smaller gift and find no joy in giving. They'll struggle to do the right thing, but they have no real target for their giving. They're focusing on the money and not the mission.

Imagine, on the other hand, that you've gone to Harry and Hermione and suggested that they make a $500,000 gift, but if the rest of the board gives another $1.5 million, they'll raise their gift to $1 million. The challenge is widely announced to the other board members. Now imagine the conversation that Donald and Dorothy might have.

Dorothy: Can you believe what Harry and Hermione are doing? They must really believe in the project. Half a million is a big gift, but $1 million— no one in town has ever heard of a gift that big.

Donald: He said he's doing it because the congregation has been growing so fast and he wants to make sure we can welcome all the new families moving to town.

Dorothy: And I also heard that although we could build the church for a little less, with $5 million, we'll have a gorgeous stained glass window— it'll feel like a real church.

Donald: You know, I was originally thinking about $100,000, but they asked us for $250,000. If we pay it over five years, we can do it, and by the time we're done, our grandchildren will be old enough to come to church with us.

The lead gift has opened up new possibilities for everyone and made it easier for others to make their gifts. Once the $250,000 gifts are made, it becomes easier to go to the other 10 board members. They will also have a reason to consider a larger gift than they might have otherwise.

Lead Gifts Can Fill Many Roles

As shown in the example above, lead gifts can serve as challenges. They show that the campaign can and will succeed.

If a lead gift comes from an unexpected source, it can also make the campaign seem broader very fast.

- Two museums in the same town were raising money for new buildings at the same time. People in town felt they had to choose sides—giving either to one or the other. Then, the chairs of one campaign gave a $1 million gift to the other institution. This generous gift meant that any talk of rivalry between the two museums was quashed.

- A social service agency was at the start of a very ambitious campaign. One of the board members was married to a wealthy man who had a reputation as a modest donor. However, because the campaign meant so much to his wife, he made a $1 million gift to the campaign as his holiday gift to her. That gift helped the campaign take off.

- A private faith-based school wasn't sure which parent they could approach for a $1 million gift to start their $13 million campaign. By chance, they talked to a single mother who shared with them how much the school had meant to her child, who was graduating that year. Her $1 million set the standard for other parents, who now felt that they could express their gratitude and hopes through a significant gift.

A lead gift from an institutional donor (a corporation or foundation) can demonstrate the value of the project to the entire community and sometimes to the entire nation.

- A hospital approached its general contractor to ask for a very large gift, although the company had never made a gift even one-fifth that size. The contractor got so excited about what the project was going to do for the community that he made the largest gift of his life. He later admitted that understanding the power of his gift helped him decide to make twice as large a gift as he had originally planned. His gift allowed a national foundation to consider a larger gift than normal.

An early lead gift can provide the working capital the project needs to stay on schedule by funding the war chest used to pay for architectural drawings, project consultation, fundraising costs, and public relations and publications. Organizations cannot 'bootstrap' their way through a campaign, one or two gifts at a time. They need the security that money in the bank provides. Lead gifts offer that.

Publicizing Lead Gifts

If you've been reading carefully, you've noticed that a lead gift doesn't do much good unless other people know about it.

Later on in this book, we'll talk about the issue of publicizing campaigns in general and why the so-called quiet phase of the campaign should actually be pretty noisy.

But for lead gifts, there are myriad reasons to spread the word.

Most donors give to help the project in any way they can. They're happy to have their gift used in the most productive manner possible.

- The parent's gift to the private school campaign was made anonymously, but the donor permitted her name to be used with any parents being asked for a gift of $100,000+. It was never announced to the general public, but influenced at least half a dozen parents to make gifts larger than what they had earlier considered

- The Seattle Symphony announced its $17 million gift nationally, helping elevate the organization to new heights and helping its campaign immeasurably.

- The husband's gift in honor of his wife was announced to the organization's annual big luncheon audience, where 1200 people heard about this extraordinary gift. It set the tone for the entire campaign of first-time, outsize gifts.

Determine who has to know about the gift and why. Figure out how to tell them. A campaign 'insiders' newsletter might tell the few people who really need to know. The regional business journal might be the proper venue for announcing a corporate gift. A special event might be the right place to publicize a special gift. Or an email to the board and steering committee might be the best route to go. Finally, in some cases, the trappings of a major press conference might be the proper response.

What Happens If You Don't Get a Lead Gift Early in the Campaign?

Sometimes your lead donor doesn't make a decision on your schedule. They aren't as close to the organization as you thought or they're going through difficult personal times and don't want to think about your project. Perhaps they've taken on responsibilities concerning another campaign.

Whatever the reason, there you are with a campaign and no place to go.

You can stop the campaign until your lead donor is ready. But that kills your momentum and wastes money. There's also no motivation for the donor to make the largest gift they can.

You can also begin putting together other pieces necessary to influence your lead donor:

- Complete the board campaign at an unexpectedly high level
- Get the editorial endorsement of your local newspaper—making sure they're only announcing the campaign, not asking people to give
- Recruit an all-star chair and steering committee
- Put together attractive and exciting named giving opportunities
- Obtain several gifts, probably from foundations or corporations, that are generous and impressive

- Create a series of 'touches' to ensure hat you can be in front of the donor as much as possible.

When the time comes to ask for the lead gift, you'll be prepared. You'll have the right strategy, the right preparation, a completely formed project team, and everything you need to encourage the prospect to make the gift of a lifetime.

What If There Is No Lead Gift?

Let's suppose you've started the campaign with the assumption that the board would give $2 million out of a $10 million campaign. They have successfully completed the board campaign, reaching $2.1 million.

You go to your first potential lead donor and ask for $1.5 million. She tells you that after careful consideration, she can give you $250,000. You go to your second potential lead donor, who was evaluated at $1 million, and request a gift at that level. "I'm sorry, but that's more than I can give, although I've thought about it and would be happy to give $150, 000," he responds. You go to your third and final lead gift prospect, who was not quite as close to the project but was perceived as having the ability to make a $1 million gift. He indicates that he'd need some time to consider the amount of his gift, but it would be no more than $250,000.

So there you are. Three wonderful, generous gifts, that represent a total of $650,000 from three prospects rated at $2.5 million. And no lead gift.

What next?

Remember the rule of 12.

Assuming that your largest board gift was $500,000, with another at $250,000, and four more at $100,000, you now have nine gifts totaling $1,800,000. Three more gifts of $250,000 would still only put you at $2,550,000. This projects to a total campaign of about $5 million—half of your goal.

So, your choices are clear:

- Analyze whether there are any prospects for gifts that would allow your top twelve to increase, thereby increasing your potential giving total

- Redo your project (after consulting your donors) to fit the new feasible campaign goal

- Determine if you can assume debt to pay off the difference between your need and what you can raise

- Consider whether any of your current donors might increase their gifts if certain considerations were met

If none of these choices work, you really only have a single choice—take a break in the campaign, determine why your feasibility study missed the mark so badly, and decide whether the campaign can be salvaged. It may be time to change consultants or volunteer leadership or both. Clearly, whatever was in place has not done the job.

- A project involved building a new headquarters for an organization to replace leased space. The new facility was to be modeled on a historic building and would cost $4 million to construct. The plans were based on the desires of a single influential board member. The feasibility study, out of concern for that person's sensibilities, did not probe deeply into public perceptions of this approach. The campaign never got off the ground. When a new consultant was brought in, the organization discovered that there were other solutions to the need for a larger, non-leased facility, including the purchase and renovation of an ideally located existing building at about half the cost of new construction. With a reduced plan, the campaign restarted and quickly gained momentum.

Sometimes, unfortunately, nothing works and you have to call it quits. How often does this happen?

In checking with firms around the country, it appears that campaigns fail less than 10% of the time. In the case of my personal experience, clients reached or exceeded their initial goal, or found a way to complete their project successfully with less money, about 93% of the time.

Whether as cause or symptom, failure to meet the "Rule of 12" was the telltale sign for each that failure was imminent.

Chapter XVI

Institutional Gifts—They're Only Individuals behind a Desk and a Set of Guidelines

"Writing Grants" Is Not Fundraising—And Usually Doesn't Work

As a board member, it's tempting to look to your staff to bring in money through writing grants. After all, there are all these institutional donors (corporations and foundations) out there just waiting for your application to come in.

They have procedures. You send in grant applications. They review them. If your grant writer knows what she's doing, your grant will get funded most of the time. You won't have to worry about talking to anyone or cultivating a stranger. All you need is the application form and a computer.

This all sounds great in theory, but it's based on faulty assumptions.

The truth is *the best grant writing in the world won't succeed if you don't do your job as a board member or campaign volunteer!*

The first thing you have to remember is that you shouldn't expect writing grants to yield a high proportion of your campaign total. When you assemble your campaign plan (Chapter VIII), corporate and foundation gifts shouldn't be the largest segments on the gift chart.

Corporations and foundations provide only a fraction of all contributions to most capital campaigns. Of all the money given away in the United States, only about 5% comes from corporations and 11% from foundations. For capital campaigns, the figures are somewhat higher (since church-related giving, almost all by individuals, skews the numbers somewhat), but still much less than half of all funds. For many projects, the percentage is extremely low—for church campaigns, independent schools, and some controversial projects, almost 100% of the funding comes from individuals. Even for social service and arts campaigns, half or more of the total raised comes from individuals rather than institutions.

Corporate Giving Is Probably Going to Stay at Low Levels

Corporate giving in the United States has been on a downward slide for decades, with small undulations. There are several major reasons for this:

- For most publicly-held companies, stockholders do not value charitable giving, since it does not directly increase profitability.

- Most corporations have gravitated toward funding programs rather than capital projects. They find that programs can offer greater recognition and more promotional value than gifts for bricks and mortar

- More and more companies have merged and acquired themselves out of local markets, so they don't feel tied to capital projects in specific communities.

- Many "new economy" technology corporations allow their giving to be employee directed, offering matches, with limits. While this results in generous total giving, it limits the potential for individual, large capital gifts.

Foundation Giving Will Continue to Grow

Foundation giving has grown over the past decades with the arrival of thousands of family foundations resulting from the new wealth of software, internet, and other industries. Starting with the Packard Foundation and continuing with the Bill and Melinda Gates Foundations, pioneers in technology have placed their wealth into charitable foundations and trusts.

In the meantime, well-managed foundations rode the stock market boom of the nineties to huge gains, which many of them consolidated before the crash of 2000–2001. All of these elements have helped push up the total amount of foundation giving—but it's still only slightly more than 10% of all funds provided to charities in the United States.

Corporations and Foundations Act Pretty Much the Same as Individuals in Their Giving

Once you accept the fact that you won't be able to base your campaign solely or even primarily on corporate and foundation gifts, there's an even bigger change in attitude required.

Simply writing grants is not the way to get gifts from corporations and foundations. *There's a magic ingredient that separates successful applications from rejected ones—you!*

Sure, your grant writer has to fill out the application.

It has to be well-written, with excellent grammar, correct punctuation and spelling. Neatness counts. You have to put forward the project in the most positive possible way and demonstrate that your goals meet the guidelines of the organization. Recognition may be important.

The major thing to remember is that institutional donors aren't faceless. There are flesh and blood people reading your grant applications. They have likes and dislikes. They're subject to the same emotions as everyone else. They help people they care about and reject those with whom they have no connection.

This translates into the same basic lesson that lies at the base of all successful fundraising:

> **People give to people and projects they know and respect. They respond to those applicants who take the time to establish relationships with them and who succeed in putting a real face on an otherwise anonymous grant application.**

Most corporations and foundations receive far more applications than they can conceivably fund. They look for reasons to eliminate organizations so that they can winnow down the applications for serious consideration. Think how much easier it is to toss your application into the rejected pile if they've never met you, never talked with you, and know none of your board members or volunteers.

Some examples may be helpful:

- A small, local maritime museum connected personally with a nationally prominent maritime enthusiast. He became friends with one of the board members and toured the museum and was impressed with its plans. He invited the museum to apply to a foundation that his father had established and the museum received a $100,000 grant. At least half a dozen other museums in the region without a connection had applied to the same foundation, without success.

- A facility that provided residential treatment for medically fragile children was in the midst of a capital campaign. They wanted to apply for a grant to a large regional foundation. Initially, the foundation was extremely negative, indicating that the project affected too few children and that the children "would never recover." The organization persevered, however, and discovered that a relative of one of its campaign volunteers sat on the foundation's Board of Trustees. He invited his curmudgeonly uncle, who crumpled when he met the kids and saw the loving care they received—and the inadequate building they were housed in. The foundation eventually made a $250,000 gift, but the real application was the visit by the volunteer's uncle.

The examples are endless. Foundations and corporations need the same attention as individuals. They are governed by human beings playing roles as executives, administrators, board members, and sometimes, even as volunteer site visitors. You have many opportunities to interact with those who make the ultimate decision—before the completed form hits the desk.

Some Basic Rules for Approaching Corporate and Foundation Funders

- Determine who the decision maker(s) is (are).

- Determine the best way to influence a positive decision. In a corporation, if there is a director of corporate giving, you should never go over their head without contacting them first. Make them your ally in approaching the chief executive—not act as if they don't matter in the process or are only a "gatekeeper".

- Share the list of decision makers with your fellow board members and volunteers and see who has connections. And don't forget, most foundations only require one board member to support a project to make sure it gets considered

- Make certain your organization fits the organization's guidelines, even if it takes a bit of explaining

- Arrange a meeting with the decision maker, involving your organization's CEO and at least one board member or campaign leader who knows them.

- Create your positioning and talking points (see Chapter XIII)

- Follow up all meetings with a phone call. The best question to ask is always "What did you think?" They'll let you know and you can respond accordingly

- Have your grant writer prepare the application, making certain that it is tailored to the funding source

- Before the application is submitted, contact your connection (email or a phone message is fine) to let them know you incorporated their thoughts into the application and that they should be expecting it soon. Make sure they receive a copy of the application.

This approach will greatly increase your chances for success in your grant applications. It will also establish relations with the funders to prepare for future support.

Once the Grant Is Submitted

Follow-up is essential once the grant has actually arrived at the funder. Again, volunteers should participate.

- A bank was considering a grant to a regional social service agency. Four separate agency board members contacted executives at the bank to tell them about other gifts that had come in and about their own support. The bank made the grant in the full amount asked for and playfully complained that they had heard from so many people they felt inundated.

- Another social service agency submitted a grant and waited four months to hear an answer. During that time, they received gifts that raised them from 40% of their goal to almost 70%, but neglected to share that information with the granting organization. They received a rejection, being told, "We didn't see enough progress toward your goal." After the fact explanations did no good and they never did receive a grant.

You should also share bad news. If you told a foundation that you hoped to receive a $500,000 gift from another funder, but only received $100,000 (or nothing), tell them. You never know how they will react. Perhaps, as often happens, they will be convinced that you really need their gift. And they will be impressed with your openness (see the discussion on transparency, in Chapter II).

Often, the funder will ask for additional information or updates. While staff is responsible for preparing those, a call from you (or email) can help at this stage. If you've gotten gifts that bring you to 80% of your goal, a short email saying "We're almost there. Your gift will get us within $100,000" will carry a lot of weight when paired with the sober analysis submitted by staff.

When You Receive Your Notification

You've worked very hard to ensure that the corporation or foundation views you as an individual with whom they have a relationship. You've tried to show them that you care about their needs and concerns. You've told them how important they are to your success.

Now's the time to prove that you mean it.

As soon as you receive an answer, respond. Call your contact and thank them.

Yes, Even if It's a Rejection, Thank Them

They've met with you, talked with you, read the application, and given your project their best thought. They deserve your thanks. You can ask what more you might have done to get support, or whether you can reapply in the future.

If it's less than what you requested, thank them profusely. They've given you as much as they think they could and should. To them, it's a generous gift. Again, don't ever fall prey to a sense of entitlement.

- A healthcare agency asked the local utility for a $50,000 gift. They received $5,000. A staff member called and asked, "Why did we receive such a small gift?" The response was predictable. The grant maker was peeved, saying that $5,000 is not small, that if the organization didn't want it, they could send it back.

- A family foundation gave $5,000 to a $14 million campaign. The organization responded with profuse, personal thanks. A few months later, they sent a follow-up thank you, letting the foundation know how the money had been used. The foundation responded by return mail with a $50,000 pledge, now satisfied that their gift would be well used.

A formal thank you is not enough. Everyone involved in the request should contact the granting agency directly, preferably through a hand-written note. The entire board of your organization should be put on alert so that they will thank any of the funder's board or staff members when they see them. It's no different than any other donor. Personal attention goes a long way toward making them want to give you a future gift—and glad that they've given you the first one.

Chapter XVII

Why the Silent Campaign Actually Makes a Lot of Noise
PR and the Successful Silent Phase

Quiet Is Not Secret

One of the few pieces of knowledge that most people possess about capital campaigns is that you don't make a public announcement until you've reached 50% of your goal. Or is it 75%? Or 90%?

They know that the period during which you're amassing board gifts, lead gifts, and assembling your various committees is known as the silent phase or quiet campaign. During that stretch of six months to two years or more, only the inner circle is supposed to know about the campaign, with details shrouded in secrecy to all but a privileged few. They believe that if you share the news several bad things will happen:

- You'll have egg on your face if things go wrong down the road and you don't make your goal.

- People will get bored hearing about the campaign.

- Talking about the campaign in its embryonic phase destroys the pleasure of surprising people about your success when you've reached a critical benchmark.

All of these things are true—but they aren't quite on target. If you remain secretive about the campaign until you reach a preset point, you run the risk of losing support, alienating potential donors, and missing the opportunity to build excitement about your project.

We have found that telling as many people as possible about the campaign is good, as long as you don't ask them to do anything!

If your hospital is planning to build a new wing, how can you not share the good news with the entire community? If your independent school plans to build an entire new upper school, how can you maintain that as a secret to all except a chosen few? If your museum is moving downtown to a larger site, why not tell the entire community and let the excitement build?

A Campaign Is a Great Time to Build Public Awareness and Let Your Potential Constituency Know What You Do

Most organizations reach only a tiny portion of their possible supporters. More than half of the households in the United States have pets, yet humane societies struggle to meet their budgets. More than half of all Americans support reproductive choice for women, yet organizations that ensure that right gain only a fraction of the population as donors.

In the past 25 years, countless organizations have defined themselves as "the city's best-kept secret." The boards of these organizations bemoaned the fact that their agency did great things, helped people, staged wonderful plays or exhibits, carried out great research—but nobody knew them.

Yet these same organizations, when it came time to launch a campaign, thought that they should keep the news under wraps until they'd reached 50% or more of their goal.

This makes no sense. If people don't know about you, why are they going to give you large amounts of money? If there isn't a groundswell of support for your cause, why should the local bank, grocery chain, or department store make a gift?

Public Awareness Creates a Positive Environment for Fundraising

Few donors make gifts only because they've seen a news spot about your organization or read an article in your local newspaper. If they've seen a spate of such coverage, however, they notice and begin to think that maybe you're an organization worthy of further investigation.

You can help this process. When your newspaper publishes a feature on how you've helped a client find a job or defeat addiction, you can send it to your top 50 potential donors with a personal note. If your local newspaper has a web edition, you can put a link to the article on your web site. You can send out an email to your top donors to alert them of upcoming TV coverage. Even if they don't watch the piece, they'll know that you're drawing attention to your good works.

If you are especially interested in generating corporate support, you have a variety of ways of reaching out to their decision makers. Most large cities have weekly or monthly business publications that are always looking for good stories. Contacting them and encouraging them to cover your activities and plans ensures your ability to reach their subscriber base.

Many cities also have a more nuts and bolts publication, a 'Journal of Commerce' that publishes public notices of contracts to let, records leases, and runs stories on pending major construction projects. If you're planning to build one of the biggest new facilities in your city (or even in your section of the city), the Journal of Commerce will want to know about it. Their readership (contractors, attorneys, accountants, and others who are connected to the construction industry) will be interested in your plans.

A detailed article will provide you with a great tool in explaining your project to potential donors. You'll be able to hand them copies of the newspaper piece and they'll see drawings, read specifications, and be impressed that your project is important enough to be in a major business publication.

Press Clippings Excite Your Board and Your Steering Committee

Everyone likes to see their name in lights. It validates their investment in a project and gives you hope that the broader community shares your enthusiasm.

Seeing a headline touting your project cannot but help build enthusiasm among your board. They no longer feel like a voice in the wilderness, crying to no one but themselves. It's easier for them to start conversations with potential donors: "Did you see the great article about the research facility in yesterday's paper? I'd love to introduce you to the scientist they featured," is an easy way to introduce someone to your organization.

Equally as important, there's something magical about having a print or broadcast reporter saying something positive about your project. For the most part, they have the credibility that will get your acquaintances to see that your passion for a new theatre or a bigger hospital is merited.

Public Awareness Starts at Home

Publicity should not be limited to broadly disseminated media. It should start with those closest to you.

Keeping in mind the need for absolute transparency, you should commit yourself to keeping anyone associated with your organization well-informed about the project. Putting out a periodic insiders' newsletter is a start. Such a newsletter can be distributed in hard copy or an email, but in all cases it should be separate and distinct, punchy, upbeat, and focused on all the good things happening within the campaign. It should allow readers to follow the project's development and success, with a special focus on your volunteer leadership.

But Won't This Make People Feel Left Out if They're Not Asked to Give?

Campaigns proceed from the top down. If you keep everyone within your community informed about the campaign, some will feel that you don't think of them as "good enough" or "important enough" to ask for a gift early in the process. For the most part, you can address this in the newsletter itself, explaining that you are approaching the board and the biggest donors first, and that you'll be talking to everyone eventually. Your basic message should be, "Your time will come."

In smaller organizations, this becomes somewhat more problematic, especially for organizations with "closed universes" such as churches and private schools. For these instances, your board members are the ones to tell their fellow congregants or parents, "Don't worry—we want everyone to give. But we're only approaching a few people now."

If someone is adamant about being among the first to give, don't refuse their gift. But make certain that they at least have the opportunity to consider a gift at the appropriate level. Preemptive gifts can cripple a campaign if they come in well below projected levels. We have found, however, that publicizing the campaign actually lessens the risk of people making unsolicited gifts. They're more likely to wait until they're asked if they know there's a defined campaign structure and schedule. If everything is rumor, they're more likely to send in an unbidden (and usually small) check.

So What's the Difference between the Quiet Phase and the Public Phase?

The quiet phase focuses on a relatively small number of donors. It aims to bring the campaign to the 'fail-safe' point, where success is absolutely assured.

If you refer to the rule of 12, you'll remember that a small number of gifts gets you to the half-way point. If you add board support to those gifts, you'll be at the 60% level by the time you complete the lead gifts phase of the campaign.

The campaign then spreads out somewhat, seeking gifts from corporations and foundations, as well as from individuals with the interest and ability to give the next level of gifts. The size of these gifts varies according to the campaign goal. For a $1 million campaign, you probably want to meet with any donor who can give $5000 or more; for a $100 million campaign, the figure may be $100,000.

The public campaign starts when you've already met with and requested gifts from most of these donors. You may be at the 60% mark at this point or the 85% mark, but the theory is the same—**going public means you're inviting everyone to give, whether they're personally solicited or not.**

Going public also means that you're telling the community that you've succeeded and that your project will be completed. You've progressed to the point where there is no way you can fail. At this point, there's no risk in giving and you're hoping that everyone will jump on your bandwagon.

Chapter XX will discuss the public phase of the campaign. For now, just remember that getting the community involved in the last 10 or 20% of the campaign will be a lot easier if you haven't kept the project a secret during the first 80 or 90%.

Chapter XVIII

Maintaining a Relentlessly Positive Outlook Reviving a Stalled Campaign— Breathing Life into your Effort without Getting Really Mad at Each Other

Campaigns Are Long

Campaigns last six months or a year or two or three years. Sometimes they last even longer. However long they last, it's a long time. Volunteers get tired, staff members wear down, and consultants find themselves out of fresh ideas.

It's easy to get discouraged and wonder whether you'll ever complete the campaign. The problem is that you expect the campaign to progress in a straight-line progression, always moving upwards and forward.

In fact, campaigns move in steps, from plateau to plateau. You work hard, money comes in. You continue to work hard, and see few results. Then after a few more months, another group of gifts arrives. Then another dry spell. At the end of the campaign, you can look back and see steady progress. But at the time, it seems like a stop and start process.

Campaigns seem long because you never see the end until it's there. You slog uphill and are always hoping to see over the crest but you just see the mountain rising in front of you. Part of the problem is that you don't feel safe until you reach the goal, because if you fall short, everyone feels the campaign has failed.

145

It's often an all or nothing feeling, with 99% representing disappointment, relief arriving only at 100%.

Good Campaigns Consist of Many Mini-Campaigns

One way of keeping campaigns fresh is to break them up into manageable pieces. First you have the board campaign, with a specific goal and timeline. Then you have the lead gifts campaign, followed by several concurrent efforts. There may be a corporate campaign and a major gifts campaign, and perhaps a public funding campaign. Each of them has a goal and a timeline, often with separate committees and volunteers and at times even different staff members.

Breaking the campaign down, using separate volunteer committees, and working with discrete goals and timelines all help keep the campaign moving and prevent burnout. But no matter how you try, the steering committee, the executive director, staff members, and consultants all are constantly looking at the totality of the campaign. The overall goal seems to stay tantalizingly out of reach, progress measurable in nano-inches.

Tempers can get frayed if overall timelines slip or gifts don't come in as quickly as predicted. Everyone is anxious and concerned when prospects refuse to make decisions or say no. When things don't go according to plan, the plan comes under question—sometimes with very testy questions.

What Difference Does It Make If People's Attitudes Get Crabby?

Campaigns are high risk. The community has you in its crosshairs of attention and some people are hoping you'll fail. Others are deciding whether they're going to give according to whether they think you'll succeed or not. Others are unwilling to make a really big gift unless they see others doing the same.

Your leaders are there for a reason. The community looks to them for signals. They want to hear from them a uniform, consistent belief that the campaign will succeed.

When your leaders express doubt, the entire community casts a negative eye on your campaign. They find reasons to put off appointments with your volunteers. They temper their enthusiasm about giving. They spread the word rapidly that "the ___ campaign is in trouble."

- The chair of a campaign had never raised money before. A lawyer, he shared his concerns about the campaign with a client. Within days, the word was out that the campaign chair was having second thoughts about the campaign and his participation in it. Quickly, the campaign unraveled, succeeding only years later. The cost of the project increased by more than $1.5 million.

- An independent school, engaged in its first-ever capital campaign, was doing very well until the school's head began expressing doubts about "whether we'll ever find the money." The volunteers took this as a sign that they were in trouble and slowed the pace of their requests. The parent body caught the negativism and held back their gifts. School alums heard about the Head's misgivings and made minimal or no gifts. The school ended up having to borrow (and pay interest on) several million dollars to complete the project.

What these instances held in common was taking concerns outside the inner circle. Tensions run high during a campaign and it is only natural to seek the cause of perceived problems.

Problems emerge when concerns leak out into the community and affect the broader perception of the campaign.

How Do You Maintain an Upbeat Attitude?

The first rule of campaigns is that outside of the innermost circle, the campaign must project an unshakeable optimism. There is never any advantage to sharing doubts about the campaign with anyone outside the steering committee.

You can't be a Pollyanna, maintaining shining happiness when you get turned down by a major donor. You do, however, have to respond with positive thinking—except within the deepest inner sanctums of the campaign.

When you get bad news, you have to ask what happened and why. You have to be willing to ask the hardest, most probing questions and be honest in your answers. Staff and consultants must be totally frank and unsparing in their discussions. We recommend that the consultant provide a confidential 'scorecard' to the board and steering committee each month to ensure that the campaign never loses its moorings.

But all of this remains in-house, under the assumption that the campaign will find a way to succeed and surmount all obstacles. You can be honest within your board and steering committee, but your goal is to craft better strategies for success. You can't compromise your potential for success by admitting doubts.

The Same Rules Apply to Decision-Making

During the course of preparing and implementing a campaign, an organization makes difficult and often contentious decisions.

- How big will the budget be?
- What will be included in the new building?
- Will you have wooden or concrete floors in your new museum?
- Will the church have stained glass windows, a double-manual organ, and a carillon?

Debate will be hot, tempers will flare, and some people will walk away after not getting their way. But everyone has to agree from the start on one incontrovertible rule:

Once the decision is made, the debate is over and the organization speaks with a single voice

Backbiting, second-guessing, and ongoing questioning are the surest path to failure. It is not easy to admit you've lost, but you have to accept the collective wisdom—and the collective wisdom is 50% of your decision making body—plus one.

The Role of the Consultant

In most campaigns, this relentless optimism pays off. You overcome doubts and questions, you get past disappointments, and more or less on schedule, complete the campaign.

Sometimes you find yourself in a position where failure seems as likely as success. How do you decide what to do?

This is why you're paying a consultant. They've done dozens or perhaps hundreds of campaigns and can assess your position from an objective, experienced point of view.

Throughout the campaign, they should have been acting as navigators of the ship, making small course corrections as needed, but generally sticking to the chosen path.

If they see that the winds have changed, the ship has veered off course, or a storm is brewing, they must feel free to share that with the organization. You have the responsibility of considering their analysis and determining what to do. Generally, they will provide you with a series of recommendations and/or choices. These might include:

- Altering the project
- Reducing the budget
- Raising the goal (the most common major change)
- Consider taking on debt
- Changing staffing
- Adding more volunteers
- Abandoning the campaign

They will also provide advice on how to relay this news to the rest of the organization and to the community to minimize negative fallout. Most of the time, the response from the community will be positive, because you'll be saying what it will take to get the project done. You'll be obeying the rule established early in this book concerning total transparency.

Stalled Campaigns

Sometimes a campaign stops dead in its tracks.

Your volunteers stop making calls. You have no more prospects. You haven't received any substantial gifts in several months. Your staff seems at a loss as to what to do next. Your consultant is repeating him or herself. The Board is worried.

Usually, this point comes when you're through with the board campaign, but have not yet completed the lead gifts portion. More rarely, it occurs when you've had a fairly successful lead gifts campaign, but the next level of donors is not responding as well as you had hoped.

Generally, you're finding that prospects are less prepared to support you then you had thought. They either make token gifts or refuse to make decisions. Your volunteers feel unable to inspire their friends and colleagues to give.

Don't Panic

If you think you're stalled, take a moment or two to analyze your position. Make sure you're not just on a plateau that will serve as a springboard to success.

Are there gifts in the pipeline, but your prospects are just taking longer than you hoped to make decisions? Have most gifts come in at the hoped-for levels, but have taken more time to develop than you expected? Have a few prospects delayed decisions, but remained interested and engaged in discussions?

Then you're probably not really stalled. You might reconsider your schedule and determine whether you can make up for lost time. You might check to make certain that you're still on a path to success. But in all probability, you'll recover and catch up to your schedule.

If You Are Truly Stalled

On the other hand, if your situation doesn't look as if it's going to get better any time soon, you have to face reality. Have you remained at the same level for more than three months (or two months for smaller campaigns)? Are you unable to see where the gifts needed to complete the campaign will come from? If a single big gift falls through, will it kill the campaign?

Then it's time for a summit meeting.

You have to gather the key players in your campaign:

- The campaign chair
- The board chair
- Your executive director

- Your chief development officer
- The campaign director
- The consultant
- The chairs of the major campaign committees

The meeting should be at a time and place where you won't be interrupted and where you are guaranteed absolute privacy and confidentiality—perhaps even secrecy. This is the one time when rules of transparency and openness don't apply. You have to have the total freedom to express yourself, vent, fret, show your fear and concern—even get angry.

You're truly at a crisis point and you can't deny it or keep it under wraps.

It's not a time to affix blame. Your purpose at this meeting is to find solutions and a path to success. If the plans you hatch here fail, then you can worry about blame—but be certain, there'll be more than enough to go around.

Use Generative Leadership

Over the past few years an understanding has emerged that boards and other volunteer groups exist as more than sounding boards to ratify staff ideas. They exist to generate new ideas and solutions. Your summit meeting is the perfect place to put this approach into practice.

To succeed, you need to frame the issue in a way that makes it easy to follow the right path. You want to ask the questions in a way that results in productive, forward-looking discussion rather than self-questioning and pessimism.

Rather than ask, "Where did we go wrong" or spend fruitless time discussing whether you can ever recover momentum, you have to find the questions that will look forward.

Keep It Simple

Good framing means that you focus on the process, not the people. You've gotten as far as you have by relying on best practices and proven approaches, by taking things in the proper order, and by allowing gifts to unfold according to their inner dynamic, not your panic.

This is no time to abandon those best practices. Instead, you have to find new ways to apply them. There are a number of productive framing questions:

- Is there any one gift that could turn the campaign around and ensure its success?

- Is there any one or two person's involvement that would jump-start the campaign?

- What hidden pockets of support have you been ignoring and how can you reach them?

- Is it time to alter the order in which you're undertaking the campaign? Would your major givers respond more enthusiastically if they knew that 5000 community members had contributed?

- Are there people who gave early in the campaign who might either connect you to their friends or consider a larger gift?

If you've reached 60% or more of your campaign, you can find a way to complete it successfully. To have reached that point means that your project is solid, it has support from people who care, and those who have invested will help you reach your goal. It might take you longer than you'd hoped, but you'll get there eventually.

- An internationally-known research center had reached about 50% of its $11 million campaign when the gifts stopped coming in. A summit identified several possible new leaders and one key donor. It also determined a path to a potential large donor who had been resistant to meeting. The campaign recruited new leaders, secured the key donation and made a connection to the large donor. The campaign eventually exceeded its goal by more than $3 million, although it took six months longer than hoped.

- A facility that provides housing for seriously ill children and their families during treatment at a local children's hospital found their campaign stalled at the 70% mark. After a lengthy and candid discussion, they uncovered the fact that they had not yet received expected support from one state within their service area. Their executive director and campaign chair traveled to that state, received a challenge gift directed at other gifts from the state, and quickly completed the campaign.

- A small hospital in a remote part of a state had completed about 60% of its campaign, although construction was well underway. The summit uncovered the fact that most of the steering committee simply didn't believe that the money was truly needed. The hospital's CEO presented the economics of the situation, which illustrated that unless the money was raised, the hospital risked bankruptcy. A successful completion to the campaign rapidly ensued.

Your summit has to be totally honest and all-encompassing. No sacred cows can go unexamined. Does the plan need changing? What more should the board chair be doing to inspire his board members? Is the consultant providing appropriate and sufficient guidance? Is anything standing in the way of volunteers making their calls?

Again, the purpose in asking these questions cannot be to skewer a guilty party. It has to be to find ways to fix the process and position the campaign for success.

Sometimes the answer can be as simple as finding the right challenge grant that can be broadly publicized and attract new gifts. Sometimes it's getting a donor to step up to an unexpected level and give the campaign an extraordinary boost. Sometimes, the two can be combined.

- A $30M+ campaign for a new theatre stalled. A local foundation with the capacity to make a $3 million gift had given a generous gift that was considerably below their capacity. The theatre dispatched the campaign chair and the managing director to meet with the foundation's administrator. A week later, the foundation announced a $2 million challenge grant, contingent on the theater meeting its goal. Revived and re-inspired, the campaign committee quickly found new donors and completed the campaign successfully.

- An ethnic museum found itself stalled after reaching the two-thirds point in their campaign. After much thought, the museum developed half a dozen "mini-campaigns" in which small groups of people worked together to earn naming or honoring opportunities on behalf of well-known members of the community. The "mini-campaigns" were under the leadership of the campaign steering committee, but brought new energy and new volunteers to the effort.

It Doesn't Take Much to Restore Hope

Campaigns are always balanced on a razor's edge. When a few gifts come in and calls go well, optimism pervades the entire apparatus. When you get several denials in a short time, your volunteers are having trouble getting appointments, and your executive director seems depressed, doubts inevitably arise.

One way of reviving a stalled campaign is to look for easy victories. Are there a few businesses that you know are going to give but have delayed approaching because their gifts won't be very large? Is there a donor who told you to "come back if you're close to your goal?" Now's the time to enlist her help. Did a newspaper reporter offer to write a story about the campaign when the time was right? Well, the time is right.

Successful campaigns are about intention. Intentions are good, but action is better. Stalled campaigns demand action. Sometimes panic spurs action, but sometimes it results in an inability to function. On the other hand, a sense of urgency combined with real progress strengthens intentions and makes success more likely.

Chapter XIX

The Major Gifts Committee and Other Committees That Ask for Gifts Face to Face

This chapter is going to be short, because it will be a recommendation to follow the advice of your staff and consultants.

We've already established that most campaigns proceed on the basis of big gifts first, then medium size gifts, and then smaller gifts. If you're working on a campaign with a goal of $5 million or more, you'll have more than 150 prospects for gifts of between $10,000 and $100,000. In large campaigns, you may have as many as 500 or 1000 prospects.

Your staff and consultant will huddle together and determine how those prospects should be divvied up and reached. They'll figure out the right mixture of volunteers and activities. Then they'll present you with a plan.

The purpose of this chapter is only to encourage you to listen to them and to remember three things:

1.   You need committees. It may seem that you don't, that if people just did what they're supposed to, you'd never have to meet. However, few individuals work as effectively on their own as in committees. And those people were great examples to inspire the rest of the committee—but only if the committee met.

2.   Committees have to meet, because the best way to get things done is through shared responsibility.

3.   Committees can't be allowed to quietly peter out; they need to be held to goals and benchmarks and to dissolve after their job is done, with appropriate fanfare to celebrate success.

The Steering Committee Can't Do It All

"How many committees do we need?" As with most questions, the answer is elusive, depending on at least three factors:

- How many identifiable layers of gifts you have between the lead gifts and the community campaign
- How big your campaign is and how many prospects you have
- How many distinct constituencies you've identified as providing the basis for gifts

Where Do We Start?

During the course of a campaign, most people will be able to establish relationships and request gifts from no more than five people.

The board chair and the campaign chair may take on two or three times that number.

In a $1 million campaign, you may have a total of 40 gifts of $10,000 or more. The first half million will come from the top 12 gifts, while the next $400,000 will come from perhaps 30 gifts. The final $100,000 will come from hundreds of gifts ranging from $25 to several thousand dollars.

In a $5 million campaign, the numbers change. You'll have 150 prospects for 100 gifts at $10,000 or more, once you've secured the 10–12 gifts that make up the initial $2.5 million. In all probability, an additional committee made up of 15 people can reach those prospects.

If your campaign is $25 million or more, you'll need more committees, because you'll have hundreds of prospects at $25,000 to $100,000, and hundreds more at $10,000–$25,000. This translates into forming both a "major" and "special" gifts committee, each of which will have 15–20 members willing to make face to face calls.

Sometimes You're Too Big to Talk to Everyone Face to Face

Larger campaigns create numbers that are too big to approach in the manner outlined above. The level at which you can hope to talk with each donor individually face-to-face rises. In a $100 million campaign, you're probably not going to be able to have a personal, one-on-one meeting with any donor from whom you'll request less than $50,000.

You'll still need committees to reach donors at $25,000, but they will be focused on discovering ways of meeting with prospects in groups. House parties, cocktail parties, hosted parties at your organization's headquarters, regional alumni gatherings—they're all approaches that allow you to invite prospects at this level to consider gifts to the campaign.

In extremely large campaigns, $25,000 gifts may be solicited by telephone, after careful cultivation by mail and other means. Prospects might not give at the level they could, but by the time you solicit them enough large gifts are in place for them to understand how their gift contributes to the goal.

This Is Where There Are So Many Possibilities, That You Have to Trust Your Staff and Consultants

The fast food outlets that let you build your own burger brag about the number of possibilities available to you. Campaigns are no different. If you have hundreds of potential donors, dozens of volunteers, scores of different methodologies to reach the donors, and eight or ten different structures to choose from, the permutations are endless.

It's your consultant's job to indicate how you should proceed. You might disagree, and that disagreement should be heard and discussed. In the end, you and your staff and consultants should make a decision that reflects the following values:

- If you believe every donor deserves individual attention, you'll need more committees

- Your respect for diversity. If you are supported by many different constituencies representing a variety of religions or racial groups, you have to find a way of reaching them in a way that respects your makeup.

- Your respect for specific supporters. If you have a strong volunteer program, you'll need a separate committee reflecting their lengthy history with the organization and their contributions to your mission.

- Your need for future volunteer-based fundraising. If you assume future volunteer-based fundraising, this is the opportunity to train several cohorts of committed volunteers.

Committees Will Overlap

You'll be raising money from the top down, but it's like a relay race. For you to move smoothly from one level of the campaign to the next, the lower level has to be in motion when they receive the handoff. Their chair has to be in place, their members chosen and at least partially trained in how to cultivate and solicit gifts, and an evaluated prospect list in place.

You'll be finishing the work of one committee when the next starts. Your lead donors will take months to make decisions. The next level, major gifts, can be asked for their gifts as long as enough lead gifts are in place to demonstrate strong support for the campaign. Campaign momentum is important, as you've seen in many of our chapters. The worst thing is for months to go by without new solicitations taking place. You want donors to feel they're making decisions on their schedules, not yours.

Chapter XX

Putting the Community into the Community Campaign—Really Going Public

Community campaigns play an important role in successful capital campaigns:

- They help make sure that everyone can give.

- They increase your organization's donor base, preparing for future annual fundraising activities.

- They offer a sense of community ownership, ensuring that many people invest in your organization's success.

- They provide your volunteers with a sense of accomplishment, because for several months your campaign becomes the talk of the town.

It is important, in most cases, not to confuse running a community campaign with actually raising money. Your community campaign will heighten community involvement and acquire new donors for the future. You also want to end the campaign on a high note, with many supporters surrounding your torchbearers as they cross the finish line.

Planning the Community Campaign

The community campaign should be part of your initial campaign plan (see Chapter VIII). You should know from the start whether you're going to include a community phase, what percentage of your total goal you expect to derive from it, and what methods you'll be using to raise those funds.

Timing

If you're going to take two years to raise $4 million, you'll probably kick off your community campaign sometime around 18 months into the campaign. If you're taking three years to raise $25 million, you'll wait until about month 28 to kick it off. In a $100 million comprehensive campaign for a college or university that might last five years or longer, the community campaign won't start until the last year.

However, working backwards from the actual start of the campaign, you'll need six months to a full year to get everything in place. You'll need printed and media materials. You may have to hire outside vendors to perform telemarketing services. You'll need to rent halls for special events, hire entertainment for concerts, or acquire underwriting for major special events.

The community campaign should have its own plan, developed by staff and your volunteers and then presented and approved by the steering committee. You should be sure that the community campaign doesn't absorb too much time from the volunteers who are pursuing large gifts, or from the executive director, who's directing the entire project. The community campaign is meant to bring you sprinting over the finish line on a high note, not staggering over exhausted and on your last legs.

How Much the Community Campaign Will Raise

Conventional wisdom used to dictate that 80% of the money comes from 20% of the donors. That seemed pretty extreme and many board members doubted it.

Well, the number is wrong. Based on hundreds of campaigns completed over the past decade, the numbers are closer to 95-5—that is, 95% of the money comes from 5% of the donors. The remaining 5% comes from the other 95% of the people who now support you or who can be attracted by the campaign.

Incomes in America have become skewed over the past several decades; the number of millionaires and multi-millionaires has sky-rocketed, while the willingness and desire of Americans to make "transformational" gifts has increased. Twenty years ago, a listing of the top 50 gifts given in America would have included donations at the $250,000 level. In 2004, a similar listing has a lower level 100 times that, with top gifts at more than $1 billion.

At the same time, competition in fundraising has increased. Donors are more selective in their giving. While most people still give to multiple organizations, responses to traditional fundraising techniques such as direct mail has declined.

Depending on your organization and the definitions you use for the community campaign, we recommend setting a goal of between 5% and 10% of the entire campaign. Less than 5% brings into question whether it's worth the effort. More than 10% is probably unrealistic except in exceptional circumstances.

If you're seeking $1 million to remodel your homeless shelter, it is likely that you'll get at least 90% of those funds through gifts that require individual approaches. You will have cherry-picked your supporters to request larger gifts from those with passion and capacity. It's unlikely there's an untapped set of donors in the community that you haven't already thought about.

Why Community Campaigns Are Expensive—But Worth the Investment

It costs more to raise a dollar during a community campaign than during any other portion of your effort. It is more labor intensive, involves more events, requires proportionally more expensive recognition (bricks, plaques) and approaches people with less previous attachment to you than any other portion of the effort.

Community campaigns seek to attract new donors, who have not given to you before. They will give smaller gifts after receiving more information than your long-time supporters. You may have to use direct mail, telephone solicitation in combination with direct mail, or other techniques to gain their contributions. All of these methods are more expensive per dollar than direct, face-to-face solicitation of people you already know.

Many community campaigns will cost as much as $.40 on the dollar for each dollar raised—that is, in a $10 million campaign, it will cost $400,000 to raise the last million dollars. You often have spent only $750,000 to raise the first $9 million. Why is it worth that much investment for the last 10% of your goal?

The answer is that you will gain 90% or more of your donors while raising the last 10% of your goal. An extraordinary benefit of the campaign will be to broaden and deepen your donor base.

These new donors represent your future. They will, if properly stewarded, become your future annual donors, event attendees, and, over time, your major donors. In seven or ten years, when you're conducting another campaign to meet community demand, those donors will be prepared to make significant gifts to support your efforts.

You shouldn't think in the short-term in relation to the cost of community campaign gifts. You will be amortizing the cost of obtaining these donors over the next decade or longer and decreasing future fundraising expenses.

Examples of Community Campaign Activities

Every time it appears that campaigns have used every conceivable fundraising approach, volunteers conjure up new ones. They find new types of events, new ways of involving more people, and new types of challenges. The following list is not meant to be exhaustive, but attempts to get your creative juices flowing in thinking about how your organization can attract new donors and complete your campaign:

- Direct mail or email to your already-existing constituencies.

- Telephone solicitation of members, alumni, patients, or other close-in constituency that have not already made larger gifts to the campaign. There are firms that do sophisticated work in this discipline. Their fees tend to be fairly high, but they reach people you wouldn't otherwise solicit.

- Well-publicized challenge grants that allow you to invite donors to give with the knowledge that their gift will leverage funds from an individual, corporation, or foundation.

- Corporate partnerships (sometimes referred to as cause-related marketing) that involve a portion of funds spent on goods or services to be donated to the campaign. A grocery store might donate five cents every time a customer purchases their proprietary brands. A bank might donate $25 for every new account that's opened during a six-month period.

- Special events tied specifically to the campaign. One organization had 35 local celebrities hand-paint ceramic masks that were then auctioned off. The buyer received a hand-painted work by the mayor or local basketball star, the "artist" got recognized for being a good community citizen, and the organization netted more than $40,000. Another organization hosted a concert by a nationally known rock group that lived in the community. A library benefited from a reading by several well-known authors who lived in the community.

- Dinner parties held by committee members, which either charge an admission fee that goes to the campaign, or else includes a solicitation. In either event, the attendees have the opportunity to visit a house they might not otherwise get to, the host is seen as charitable, and the organization gains considerable money.

- The sale of bricks, pavers, or other permanent recognition. These have been popular in many places, but appear somewhat less popular now. The primary challenge is setting the price high enough to cover the costs of inscribing the bricks and marketing the opportunity.

- Cans on countertops. This is low cost, but difficult to administer and requires excellent logistical support.

There are dozens (or hundreds) of other ideas. Have a brainstorming session, where you assemble your most imaginative volunteers. List all their ideas and then have the community campaign committee evaluate them. They should choose the best opportunities to increase your donor pool, raise money, and prepare you for the future. They should also evaluate the amount of work required and ensure that the ideas can be implemented without draining the organization.

Public Awareness

The community campaign is the one time when you want the absolute maximum possible amount of press coverage. While it should be targeted toward your best prospects, you shouldn't be concerned about getting coverage that's too broad. You're in a small town, but a metropolitan TV station wants to cover you—great. It won't hurt for people in the big city to hear about your plans.

The community campaign is a great time to bring in a media sponsor, who'll run your ads for free, tell their readers, listeners, or viewers about your campaign, and even help sell your mementos. They can advertise your events, feature interviews with your staff and clients, or do awareness building.

- A local ad agency developed a series of ads featuring "kids fighting cancer," on behalf of a Ronald McDonald House. The local cable networks picked them up and ran them for a year. The total value of air time for the spots exceeded $1 million.

- A newspaper adopted a campaign by the local zoo to build a new elephant house. It featured the campaign on an almost daily basis, ran clip-out coupons soliciting donations, and reported on campaign progress.

- A weekly newspaper sponsored a campaign by a small homeless shelter to expand. They ran an update in each issue, featuring a full page that discussed the campaign, featured a local donor, and encouraged people to donate.

Famous Chairs

The community campaign is the right place to install as chair a well-known person who's reluctant to ask for money face-to-face.

Your local baseball star, anchorwoman, bestselling author, or other celebrity can lend credibility to the campaign and attract others to the effort. His or her presence at a special event can increase attendance; their signature on a direct mail appeal can attract attention. Their face on a billboard or a television ad can make sure your message is seen and heard.

If you wish to recruit a celebrity as a spokesperson or chair of your community campaign, there are only a few things to make certain they agree to:

- Like every other leader, they have to make a gift to demonstrate that this really is something they care about.

- They have to project the right image for your organization.

- They have to be clear what they're agreeing to, in terms of use of their name and image, tasks to be performed, and events to attend.

- They have to be clear about the amount of time they are willing to commit and the types of activities they are willing to undertake.

For many organizations, you're better off having a well-known, highly respected citizen as your community campaign chair. If your church has a member who helped found the congregation 60 years ago and still shows up every Sunday, she's perfect! If your humane society has a supporter who's well-known throughout the community as a leader and a volunteer, he's a great chair!

Such people convey the concept that you're credible and connected to the community. They're believable because they walk the walk of community service. They're also accessible and just "plain folks," sending out a positive message about how your organization regards its grassroots supporters.

Sometimes, you'll be best off recruiting someone attached to the mission of your organization. The library might have a children's book author chair the community campaign. A beloved pediatrician is a great community campaign chair for a hospital. Accessibility, credibility, connection. Strive for those and you'll be better off than seeking fame, fortune, and fandom.

Make Sure It's Fun

The lead gift and other portions of your campaign are seldom vehicles for true fun. You're talking to people about their deepest values and helping them make decisions that are sometimes life-changing.

Your relationships are enjoyable, you can feel joyful about the process in which you're engaged, but you're not very often having fun in the normal use of the word. Donors are looking deep into their own souls, often in private or with the help of a trusted counselor. Eventually, they'll celebrate and rejoice in their gift, but ordinarily not while they're thinking about it.

The community campaign is different. You are trying to attract new people to your organization. Part of the reason they'll decide to join you is their perception that you represent an enjoyable, 'fun' group of people who understand that life is not always a life or death situation. During the community campaign, only a fraction of the gifts are of the variety that requires either deep thought or deep conviction. They're 'heart' gifts, rather than emanating from reason. You want to do something to keep the cute cat from being euthanized; you want to help the inner city kid attend camp; you want old people to have loving care in their declining years.

Community campaign donors make gifts that they can pay off with relative ease, often by writing a check or putting it on their credit card. The majority of community campaign gifts are $250 or less, a size that is generous, but falls into "ongoing discretionary expenditures," rather than a major gift from assets.

In return, you are offering a sense of satisfaction and enjoyment. If the donor attends an event, the emphasis should be on fun. If they are invited to buy something, there should be a sense of playfulness and fun in the invitation.

The committees involved in raising money during the community campaign should focus on fun as well. Make the meetings more like parties than the serious, straight-laced gatherings that governed the lead gift efforts. Serve some wine, meet at people's houses or clubs, and spend some social time around each meeting.

The community campaign is when you'll touch the most people both as donors and as volunteers. You'll be laying the foundation for long-term financial health based on an expanded support base. Make sure that they are left with a good feeling and the desire to come back for more.

Part Three:

After the Campaign Is Over

Chapter XXI

Celebrating Your Success

All Good Things Must Come to an End

At some point, you have to say "done" and mark completion. Whether you're at goal, $150,000 away from it, $500,000 beyond it with money pouring in, there's a point at which the campaign is over.

There are two reasons campaigns must come to a clearly defined close:

- Your volunteers have signed up for a limited commitment, not a life sentence

- The community heard you set a goal and a timeframe. They want you done so the next project can take center stage.

When a campaign drags on, you're violating a trust that you've established with your supporters. You're putting into question your willingness to play by the rules.

When Is the Campaign Over?

If you've raised enough money to complete your project (whether you've reached your goal or not) and your volunteers' energy is flagging, it's time to stop.

If you've reached your goal, even before the campaign is scheduled to end, it's probably time to stop unless you have a very good, mission-based reason to continue. If raising more money will allow you to increase services by cutting debt service, it might be a reason to continue until you're scheduled to end. But raising money after your goal is reached makes you appear greedy in the eyes of the community and puts you in a position of "hogging the wealth."

It's time to stop if you've reached your goal and the campaign time has run out, even if you think you could raise more. As is the case in show business, it's always good leaving them wanting more rather than wearing out your welcome. Just be sure you continue to talk to the prospective donors you haven't yet reached.

How to Celebrate

You have three separate ways to celebrate.

The first is the internal celebration for the folks who made it happen—you and your board colleagues, your executive director and staff, your committee members, the consultants, architects, and everyone else who made your success possible.

Use the celebration to achieve closure, to thank them, to acknowledge their hard work, and to give thanks for your success. This celebration is the smallest, and can be the most intimate and enjoyable, because you can let your hair down. You can roast the campaign chair, share horror stories of the campaign, and admit your fears and concerns. You've won. Your only concern is that those who were integral to the campaign feel appreciated for their work. This celebration should be the first and should allow those most closely involved in the campaign to have the first glimpse of the finished project. They should be treated as the ultimate insiders, given a behind the scenes tour.

The second celebration is for your donors, your staff, and volunteers—both those who helped with fundraising and those who help you keep your doors open every day. It's a time to thank everyone who's gotten you to the point where you can open the doors to your new facility—or start drawing money from a larger endowment.

Your volunteers should meet the donors and thank them for their monetary contribution. The donors should meet your staff and volunteers so that they understand who's responsible for making sure their investment is well used. The grateful patient who gave the money for a new operating suite should meet the surgeons who'll be using it, as well as the nurses who'll make certain he's well-tended during the operation.

The third celebration is for everyone—the entire community. This celebration should feature a very short program to thank those who made the successful campaign possible, but should focus on a celebration of this great gift to your community. The point is not that Mrs. X is a generous patron of the arts, it's that your community now has a modern art museum that has the climate control system needed to host major traveling art exhibitions. The celebration is not for demonstrating that Mr. Y showed great leadership during the campaign, but rather that your city now has a new library that's "as exciting a place for kids as the street," as one donor characterized her dream.

This celebration should be all-encompassing, involving as many people as your facility can hold (assuming it's held at your building. If you can't host it at the facility (e.g. it's a confidential shelter for battered women), then celebrate elsewhere.

A celebration makes more people aware of your mission-based activities. It brings in new people and introduces them to committed staff, volunteers, and donors. It gives your volunteers the chance to bask in the community's admiration. It also marks the moment when the campaign is absolutely done and you can start preparing for the next one.

- A regional art museum held a 24-hour opening, turning the celebration over to various groups for an hour or two at a time. More than 7000 people showed up, keeping the museum humming with activity for the entire day and introducing a broad swathe of the community to the facility.
- A theatre with three separate auditoriums staged a rolling party that took people from one venue to the next, with performances at each place, allowing thousands of people to get a small taste of live theatre in a beautifully restored building.

What about a Gala?

The celebrations described so far are a legitimate part of the fundraising campaign and the cost should be absorbed by the campaign. You can have a no-host bar if you want to recover some money and you can open up your gift shop for a special preview. But you're defeating the purpose of your celebration if you charge $500 (or even $100) for admission.

A gala is for a different purpose.

You stage a gala when you've created something really special, when the building itself is going to be an attraction and where you're hoping that the site itself will be an attraction in the future. Whether it's a world-class library designed by a great architect, or a state-of-the-art hospital with gleaming lobbies and new services, your new building deserves a celebration.

You can charge for this, because you're giving people a first look at your new building, an insider's glimpse of what all the hoopla has been about. The gala can be for people who'll pay for the privilege of a first look.

A Gala Should Make Money

If you're going to the trouble of staging a gala, with Klieg lights, musicians, good food, fancy wine, perhaps a well-known entertainer, you're going to have to spend a wad. Get underwriters to cover your costs—they'll want to be associated with a winner, and it's a good way to attract some corporations that want high visibility but aren't especially charitable.

Charge enough to make a tidy profit—maybe the equivalent of a couple of month's operating reserves. If you can get all your expenses covered and then sell 50 tables at $2500 each, you have a $125,000 cash infusion. If you're a theatre with a $1 million operating budget, you've just created a great cushion to kick off operations in your new facility. This obviously won't work for a hospital, but you can set lofty goals nonetheless.

People love a party, and having it at a gleaming new site that the entire community has come together to build is a good thing.

Chapter XXII

Stewardship—Or the Last Day of the Campaign Is the First Day for Your Reborn Organization

Your Capital Campaign Donors Are Your Future

The campaign is over. You've celebrated, reveled, relaxed. You wake up in the morning and you no longer have to ask yourself, "Will we make it?" You've reached your goal, the building is built or nearly so, the endowment is invested with policies in place, and the entire community has breathed a sigh of relief.

From the point of view of your donors, the campaign has really just begun.

Depending on the size of your campaign, between a few dozen and several hundred people have just made the largest gifts of their lives. They've invested enough in your project to have had a great vacation, a new car, or even a new house.

They have made those gifts in the belief that they would achieve a goal of importance to them. Their gifts reflected their most deeply-held, personal values. They believe in the education your independent school is offering to Catholic girls. They believe in the importance of art to a vibrant downtown. They have a passionate concern about the homeless, the mentally ill, or the at-risk kids of your community.

They haven't given to a building, or an endowment, or anything concrete or financial. They've given to something more precious—the ability to achieve change in your community.

They will continue to support your mission and protect their investment as long as they are convinced that you bring their ideals and values to life. If you maintain and improve the quality of education at your school, attract the best physicians and nurses to the hospital, provide loving respectful care to the community's elders, they will want to see you prosper. They will continue to support you financially and as your representatives in the community.

Some will join your board.

Some will volunteer for committees.

Some will talk about you at the Rotary Club or at their golf club.

Some will help you gain access to other leaders.

None of this will happen unless you are accountable.

At the very start of this book, in the discussion of ethical fundraising, ethical element III stated, *"Your organization should be totally accountable for all money received."*

Accountability means a lot of things to donors. It means that you should report back to them how the campaign has gone. Did you reach your goal? Stay under budget? If not, why not?

It also means that they want to know you're protecting their investment. If you've established an endowment, how is it being invested? What sort of return will you get? What are the fees charged?

But most of all, accountability is about your ability to deliver your mission. You promised that your campaign would allow you to reach more people, serve them better, and perhaps offer new services. Has that happened? How can you demonstrate that you are reaching more people in more effective ways? Did you establish evaluation procedures and standards?

You have to be willing to share your outcomes with your donors. You made projections about your first-month attendance or client growth. You should share your results with your donors. <u>That's</u> what they've paid for.

- A small hospital added a birthing center. They had projected that there would be about 40 births during its first month of operations. Instead, they had more than 60. They sent out notes to all their donors informing them of this success, delighting them with the center's debut.

- A 100-year old independent school rebuilt its lower school, which had suffered from falling enrollment for almost a decade. In the first year it opened its new campus, both new enrollment and retention jumped markedly. The school's annual campaign had one of its best years.

Capital and Endowment Gifts Are Part of the Giving Cycle, Not Ultimate Gifts

The worst mistake that you can make is to assume that's someone's gift to your campaign is their final gift to you. Would you buy a new house and then stop putting money into it for maintenance and modernization? No—it would remain the biggest recipient of your expenditures on living expenses.

Your nonprofit organization is no different. You've spent months or years developing a relationship with a donor. This relationship was not based on a single gift—it was based on creating an ongoing commitment and partnership that would ensure that both you and the donor feel gratified by the progress your organization is making.

As time goes on, your major donors should deepen their relationship with you, not abandon it. They should feel that they are part of your family, entitled to frequent reports on your progress and privy to your family secrets. Your major donors are fully aware that in most cases you can't survive without ongoing support. They should be part of your future celebrations and successes, as well as your confidants when things are not going well.

Part of Accountability Is Transparency

Ethical fundraising requires that you be open and honest about your organization. You can't hide the bad or mask disappointments. Your donors deserve an honest, complete report. They have your best interests at heart and will not try to apportion blame—if they're not surprised.

- A social service agency developed a new model of care for foster children. They attracted several large gifts and began plans to build a large rural campus. Unfortunately, they ran into both licensing and permitting problems on both the state and local level. They did not share the bad news with donors until it was too late. This failure ruptured their relationship with their largest donor, who could have helped them solve some of their problems had she known about them.

More and more, major donors see themselves as actively involved in the organizations they support. They don't want to meddle in the organization, but they want to feel useful. Unless they know your challenges, they can't help you. By denying them that opportunity, you are missing an opportunity, as well as implying a lack of trust in their fidelity to you.

- Shortly after an organization finished a major campaign and had moved into its splendid new building, they discovered that their bookkeeper had stolen a sizable amount of money. They immediately shared this news with their board, their biggest donors, and other valued supporters. They also pursued the employee with the full weight of the law, in a very public manner. They introduced new controls to prevent it from happening again. They didn't lose any support or major annual donors.

Bad things happen to everyone. Your donors are attracted to you because they feel needed, but also because they know you're willing to take chances. They will forgive you for failures and mistakes, as long as you show a willingness to learn from them. Most donors are aware that "Even Babe Ruth struck out 2130 times."

Always expect your donors to support you in hard times if they have the opportunity. Don't "spare them bad news" or "save them for when you really need them." Let them be part of your organization on an ongoing basis, so that they are never surprised or feel that I'm "the last to know."

Share good news as well. Your faithful supporters and board members should be the first to know when you receive a big grant. They should be in the lead position to thank the donor and tell others your success.

Good Stewardship Costs Money

Most of this chapter is to convince you that when the campaign is over, contacts with donors must go on. Your organization needs to remain in close touch with them, to ensure that they will continue to be your first line of support in the future.

That takes staff time, materials, and technology infrastructure. You have to have an interactive Web site, frequent emails, and phone calls and notes from the organization. You need to pay for an audit and include its major findings in a printed annual report. You need to gather your important donors for advisory meetings and updates, and show them your hospital's new equipment, your school's new laboratory, or your agency's new programs.

In general, if you have an active, ongoing fundraising program that follows on a capital campaign, you need to retain a full-time staff person for approximately every 200 major donors you wish to retain contact with. This professional development staff person will not only pay for herself, but will generate increased revenue over time. Her contribution will be quantifiable and predictable, assuming you and your fellow board members perform your tasks.

Fundraising Is Always a Team Sport

When the campaign is over, your job starts again. You are responsible for maintaining the relationships that you generated during the course of the campaign. Your staff members can support these activities, but if one of your friends has made a $500,000 gift to help build a local Boys and Girls Club, it's your job to keep them connected. They need to know the outcome and your successes. You're the one to invite them to your auction, bring them in during your town's "Day of Caring," and otherwise deepen their relationship with your organization.

You are their peer. No matter how mature and skilled your development staff members are, they cannot take your place. All of the same reasons why you had to be part of all campaign requests factor into why you provide the lead during stewardship efforts.

Afterword

The Afterglow
What It Will Feel Like
When You're Done

Only the Success Sticks in Your Mind

In the late 1980s, a museum raised the equivalent of its annual budget to host an international exhibit of contemporary art.

The board had never raised money before. The town was in the midst of a two-decade decline that left its downtown in shambles and residents fearful of coming downtown at night. The art itself was difficult, forbidding, and everything else that most people associate with contemporary art. Even someone with a Ph.D. in cultural history was hard-pressed to grasp what the curator was trying to say in his catalog.

Despite all of these obstacles, a dedicated group of passionate leaders persevered. They raised more than $800,000 in six months and brought the exhibit to the Museum. Even before it opened, the show caused a sensation with glowing articles in regional and national media. The exhibit eventually provided the springboard to build a new museum and reinvigorate the entire downtown core.

At the opening itself, the board members sipped expensive liquor donated by a local distributor who'd never been inside the museum before. More than 500 people milled around, expressing their delight, indignation, disgust, or outrage at the art, but all feeling proud that it was <u>here,</u> not in a large museum 40 miles away.

In the midst of this, three board members who'd been the hardest to convince of the show's merits or the advisability of doing it stood celebrating. They solemnly raised their glasses to each other and the oldest, most curmudgeonly, said, "Well, we showed them. We did it!"

Success

How many times in your life can you feel that you've done something that mattered? Your children's birth, their graduations and weddings, landing a good job, buying your first house are all satisfying. But they're private and have more to do with your personal goals than with contributing to the overall community welfare.

A successful capital campaign introduces success of a different magnitude. You've been a vital part of something that will affect others for as long as you and your children live. Your name will be inscribed on the building's walls and will be inseparable from its activities as long as it stands.

In the course of a campaign, you've surprised yourself with your courage. You've stepped outside your comfort zone and suddenly found yourself as a leader. You took a risk and were rewarded.

We know about Carnegie because of his libraries. But we also know wealthy people in our own cities and towns who are revered and respected because of what they've done for the community's institutions. When you've played a significant role in building a new hospital, YMCA, church, theatre, school, or any other building that changes lives, you will feel a sense of satisfaction unlike almost any other. You can feel pride and accomplishment. You've faced great challenges and overcome them and now you can bask in the sense that you've completed your job.

You've Brought a Vision into Being

Two or three or perhaps five or more years ago, you were part of a group of people who embarked on a campaign motivated by a vision. You imagined what it would be like to have a hospital on your side of the bridge or a full-size YMCA with a swimming pool for your kids. You heard all doubts and felt all the nervousness surrounding such a bold undertaking.

But you were a leader, one of the brave and selfless. You helped plan the project. You tested it within the community. You guided it over years of difficult decisions and times when things were uncertain at best. You made the largest gift of your life and invited others to do the same. You watched the new building take shape and celebrated its completion.

How many people have had the satisfaction of watching a new building fill for the first time, of seeing kids crush into a new gym, or theatre-goers exclaim over the plush seats in the theatre you helped create? How many people can take their grandchildren to a community landmark and tell them, "Thirty years ago, I helped make this possible"?

For the rest of your life, you'll have the memory of looking at the new building, or the renovated wing, or seeing the first scholarship awarded from the endowment you helped raise. You'll always know that you did something that made a difference and that took true commitment. It will give you the confidence to take on other tasks and ensure that you have something to answer when you ask yourself, "What have I accomplished in this long life of mine?"

Others see you as someone who gets things done and who doesn't shy away from the tough tasks. Remembering what you've done can be a present to yourself for the rest of your life. Enjoy it. On a larger or smaller level, you're a hero. You deserve everyone's thanks.

Appendices

APPENDIX A:

Sample Budget Sheet for Project Costs

PROJECT DEVELOPMENT	
CONSTRUCTION SOFT COSTS	
Project Planning Fees	
Architectural Design Fees	
Architectural Consultants (e.g. interior design, acoustical	
Engineering Fees	
Redesign Fees (if applicable)	
Land Acquisition Costs	
Exhibit Design (if applicable)	
Site Survey/Site Preparation	
Project Administration - Internal*	
Project financing	
(___% interest plus fees on $___ million for ___ years)	
Other	
SUBTOTAL:	$0.00
CONSTRUCTION HARD COSTS	
Construction Costs: _____ s.f. @ $____ per s.f.	
General Contractor Construction	
Sales Tax	
Construction/Structural Testing	
Demolition	
Telephone/Computer Networking System	
Furniture, Fixtures & Equipment	
Landscaping	
Permanent Donor Recognition (hard costs: e.g. donor wall, plaques)	

Construction Contigency @ Escalation @ ___% annually through midpoint of construction	
Other	
SUBTOTAL:	$0.00
* If additional staff must be hired to implement the project during design and building.	
PROJECT SOFT COSTS	
Permits/Fees	
Hook-up Fees/Utilities	
Construction & Liability Insurance	
Performance Bond	
Relocation Costs (including transition)	
Real Estate Property Taxes During Construction	
Appraisal (for construction loan)	
Owner's Representative/Project Management	
Financing Costs	
- Closing Legal	
- Title Insurance	
- Environmental Assessment	
- Closing Costs	
- Lender's Inspection	
Project Contingency (Miscellaneous)	
Other	
SUBTOTAL:	$0.00
FUNDRAISING BUDGET	
Campaign Personnel	
Infrastructure/Resources	
Professional Fees	
Materials	
Campaign Meetings/Events	
Donor Recognition	

SUBTOTAL:	$0.00
* Fundraising costs typically account for up to 20% of the total budget.	
Other	
Summary Budget	
Construction Soft Costs	
Construction Hard Costs	
Project Soft Costs	
Fundraising Budget	
Other	
SUBTOTAL:	$0.00
TOTAL CAPITAL PROJECT COSTS:	$0.00

APPENDIX B:

Sample Campaign Materials Worksheet

TYPE	QUANTITY	STATUS	TIMELINE	COST
MATERIALS BUDGET: To be determined (estimate $35K to $80K (without video, software or website upgrade))				
DONOR RECOGNITION BUDGET: $15K - $25K minimum (to be determined)				
STATIONERY:				
Letterhead	5,000-10,000			
2nd page	10,000-20,000			
Envelopes	5,000-10,000			
Thank you cards/env.	2,500 – 5,000			
Mailing labels	2,500-5,000			
Large Envelopes (prospectus/proposals)	1,000-2,500			
Pledge cards (triplicate)	1,000 – 2,500			
Return Env. (BRE) (depending on structure of community campaign)	5,000 – 20,000			
SUBTOTAL				
MAJOR GIFTS AND PRESS PACKETS				
Viewbooks – (approx. $15 each)	200 – 500			
Press packets	100			
Presentation Folders	500 – 1,000			
SUBTOTAL				
BROCHURES				
Major Donor (optional, depending on viewbooks)	2,500 – 5,000			
Community Campaign (TBD)	5,000 – 20,000			

SUBTOTAL				
NEWSLETTER				
20 issues (approx. 10/year)	500 to 1000 each edition			
OTHER:				
SUBTOTAL				
TOTAL MATERIALS	$35K – 80K **(without video, software or website upgrade)**			$35K – 80K

CAMPAIGN DONOR RECOGNITION WORKSHEET

DONOR RECOGNITION	TBD			$15K-$25K (Min.)
Pins, etc.				
Pavers				
Plaques				
Other				
TOTAL				

VIDEO & WEBSITE/SOFTWARE UPGRADE WORKSHEET

TYPE	QUANTITY	STATUS	TIMELINE	COST
VIDEO	(optional)			
Major donors, community mtgs	100 – 500			
Other (bus signs, etc.)				
SUBTOTAL				
DONOR SOFTWARE PURCHASE OF UPGRADE				
SUBTOTAL				
WEBSITE				
Creation/upgrade				
Maintenance				
Addition of campaign pledge information				
SUBTOTAL				

APPENDIX C:

Sample Job Descriptions

CAMPAIGN CHAIR
SAMPLE JOB DESCRIPTION

Timeline:

Expectations:

Work with a team of staff, fundraising counsel and a network of community volunteers to *lead* the campaign:

- Chair meetings of the Steering Committee

- Help establish and monitor campaign policies and progress

- Maintain frequent contact with staff and campaign counsel to preserve momentum, review strategy and implement decisions

- Recruit and solicit additional campaign leadership

- Work with all committees to assist in identifying prospects and tailoring strategies

- Identify potential donors and approach peers for campaign gifts (initial focus on pledges of $50K+)

- Encourage campaign workers at all levels

- Serve as key spokesperson at events and in news stories, and be a constant, positive representative for the campaign

- Make a campaign gift that is significant for you.

Membership:

The full steering committee consists of 8 to 12 volunteer leaders. The steering committee will be supported by a sub-committee structure involving as many as 25 to 50 campaign volunteers.

Estimated Time Commitment:

Approximately 3 to 5 hours per month is required for monthly steering committee meetings, overseeing sub-campaign chairs and fundraising calls. From time to time, a separate campaign co-chair briefing may be scheduled to discuss specific overall campaign strategies or issues that need to be addressed.

Board Gifts Task Force
Sample Job Description

Timeline:

Expectations:

The Board Gifts Task Force Committee provides leadership for the Board Campaign, setting the tone and expectations for the overall campaign. A committee of board members will work with staff and The Collins Group to:

- Shape board campaign to establish stretch goal and 100% participation
- Identify appropriate, respectful request levels for board members to reach that goal
- Make stretch campaign gifts that are significant for them
- Approach peers for stretch campaign gifts
- Be a constant, positive representative for the campaign

Membership:

Chair plus two to four additional trustees as committee members.

Estimated Time Commitment:

Two to three task force meetings, plus personal and team solicitations of board members.

Campaign Steering Committee
Sample Job Description

Timeline:

Expectations:

Work with a team of two to three campaign co-chairs, staff, fundraising counsel, and a network of community volunteers to *lead* the capital campaign:

- Help establish and monitor campaign policies and progress
- Identify and recruit additional campaign leadership
- Play a key role in a campaign sub-committee or task force
- Identify potential donors, open doors and/or approach peers for campaign gifts
- Make a campaign gift that is of significance to you
- Maintain regular contact with staff and counsel to preserve momentum
- Be a constant, positive representative for the campaign

Membership:

The full steering committee consists of 15 to 20 volunteer leaders. This group will be supported by a sub-committee structure involving as many as 25 to 50 campaign volunteers.

Estimated Time Commitment:

The full steering committee meets monthly. Approximately 1.5–3 hours per month is required plus fundraising calls.

APPENDIX D:

Sample Gift Chart

Gift Chart for a $10 Million Capital Campaign

Size of Gift	# of Gifts Needed	Category Total	Running Total
$2,500,000	1	$2,500,000	$2,500,000
$1,000,000	2	$2,000,000	$4,500,000
$500,000	3	$1,500,000	$6,000,000
$250,000	6	$1,500,000	$7,500,000
$100,000	9	$900,000	$8,400,000
$50,000	12	$600,000	$9,000,000
$25,000	15	$375,000	$9,375,000
$10,000	20	$200,000	$9,575,000
<=$5,000	Many	$425,000	$10,000,000
Total		$10,000,000	

APPENDIX E:

Call Preparation

BEFORE YOU MAKE YOUR CALL:

1. Focus on the mission—not yourself, not the money, not the capital or endowment projects.

2. By far, the best way to raise money is to ask for it in a face-to-face situation. The purpose of the call is to get a meeting.

3. Don't hear no unless they say no. Almost everyone will offer some resistance.

4. You don't have to know everything to talk to people. You can get back to them later with answers.

5. There are no magic words. Your commitment and your passion for the project are the most convincing aspects of the solicitation.

6. Be prepared to listen. People will usually tell you what they want to be asked for.

7. If pairing with another volunteer, decide who is going to actually make the request and for how much. Be familiar with all the recognition opportunities including named gifts.

8. Be aware of ways to make people's giving easier: three-year pledges, appreciated assets, real estate, planned gifts.

9. Don't make people's decisions for them. Let them decide how much they want to give.

10. Never contradict or argue. You are building a relationship, not selling a product.

11. If people are not ready to make a commitment, treat the call as the first step towards a successful solicitation.

12. Every gift is a good gift.

APPENDIX F:

Sample Org Chart

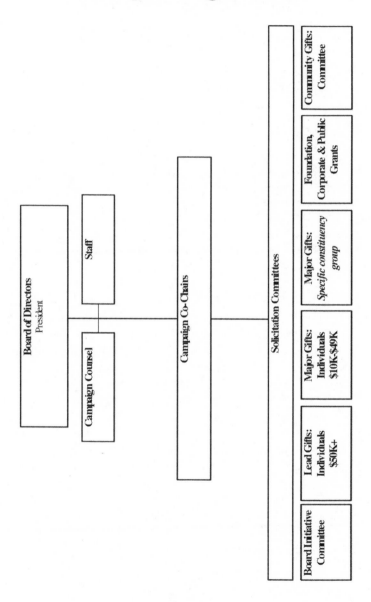

APPENDIX G:

Sample Pledge Form

Insert
Logo

CAPITAL CAMPAIGN GIFT
[Insert Project Description]

DONOR INFORMATION (please type or print)   Date: _____

NAME _____

ADDRESS _____

CITY _____ STATE _____ ZIP _____

TELEPHONE (HOME) _____ BUSINESS _____ FAX _____ EMAIL _____

PLEDGE INFORMATION

In consideration of the gifts of others, I (we) hereby contribute cash and/or assets to [Organization Name].

I (we) pledge a total of $_____ enclosed $_____ pledged $_____

Please bill me beginning _____ and thereafter ☐ monthly ☐ quarterly ☐ yearly ☐ other _____

I (we) wish to have this donation spread over ☐ 1 ☐ 2 ☐ 3 years(s) ☐ other _____

My gift will be matched by _____ company/foundation/family.

       ☐ Form enclosed ☐ Form will be forwarded

☐ I (we) would like information on including [Organization Name] in my (our) will/estate planning.

CONTRIBUTION FORM

I (we) plan to make my (our) contribution in the form of ☐ cash ☐ check ☐ charge ☐ stock ☐ property ☐ other _____

Please charge my credit card (circle one) VISA / MC number _____ exp. date _____

    Authorized signature _____

LISTING (Donors will be recognized in campaign materials unless an anonymous gift is requested).

Please use the following names(s) in all acknowledgments _____

_____

Signature(s) _____ Date _____

Please make checks, corporate matches, and stock transfers payable to: [Organization Name]

Donations are tax-deductible to the extent allowed by the law.
Mail your pledge to: [address]

For more information, contact [Contact Name], [Title]
Phone [　#　] • fax [　#　] • [email] • [website]

978-0-595-41472-7
0-595-41472-9